BEGINNING MEDIUMSHIP WORKBOOK
How to Develop your Mediumship Skills

Carole Anne

ISBN: 9781730947728

Contents

BEGINNING MEDIUMSHIP WORKBOOK

Welcome to "Beginning Mediumship Workshop"

My aim with this book is to help you expand your psychic awareness and mediumship ability. I have called this book Beginning Mediumship Workbook because I am including material I use in Mediumship Workshops with examples of feedback and questions from students that might help you understand your own responses and experiences as you work your way through the book and the exercises within the book. This is one of a number of Psychic Training Programs focused on your spiritual growth and development.

In this book/workshop, I will introduce you to your different intuitive, spiritual and psychic gifts and how to build your mediumship skills.

This will include:

• How to prepare yourself for mediumship
• Awareness of your energy field
• How to establish a link with spirit and enhance the spiritual link by sitting in the power
• How to understand the symbolic language of Spirit
• Practice on building evidence based spirit messages
• How to trust your ability to receive spirit
• Exercises on how to develop your mediumistic ability

I hope you enjoy and look forward to sharing with you.
Love & Light, Carole Anne

What is a Medium?

A lot of people ask: what is the difference between a medium and a psychic? So, I feel this is a good place to start.

I believe that everyone has psychic abilities to a degree, even those who don't recognise or use them. A psychic is someone who is sensitive to nonphysical forces. Psychics are able to perceive information through their 'sixth sense', or extra sensory perception. A medium has learned to use their psychic side to connect with the spirit world. All mediums are psychic, not all psychics are mediums.

Some techniques mediums use to link with spirit are:

(a) Intuitively linking with the feelings of the person being read and the spirit around them. This ability is known as clairsentience ··· like when you meet someone for the first time and just get a 'feeling' about them that usually turns out to be right. Drawing on this 'feeling' ability to receive information, a medium can then move deeper to bring information from the spirit world.

(b) By 'seeing' spirit. Psychic information that comes through visually is known as clairvoyance. It's a bit like seeing things in our imagination only the medium isn't making up the images, they are receiving them from an outside source. In this, mediums might 'see' images or flashes of images in their head. They aren't necessarily 'seeing' spirit standing in front of them as many people believe.

(c) Mediums who are also psychics often use tools such as crystal balls, tea leaves, scrying mirrors, pendulums, runes or cards to receive psychic insights, however, the tools can also act as a trigger that lifts the reading to a mediumistic level and brings forward spirits.

(d) Through creating a place in their minds where they can connect with their guides and with spirit.

Information comes to mediums in different ways and there are many different types of mediums including: Psychic Mediums who use their psychic powers in mediumship; Trance Mediums who allow spirit to speak directly through them and Spiritualist Mediums: Mediums who are also Spiritualists. This Workbook will be looking at how to prepare yourself for mediumship and how to practice mediumship using your psychic abilities.

Mediumship Workshop – Part 1 – Preparing yourself for Mediumship

Preparing for Mediumship 1

Why do I want to be a Medium?

Before starting on mediumship perhaps the first question you might ask yourself is: Why do I want to be a medium?

As a medium you are being 'of spiritual service'. Your commitment to this should be sincere, with a humble attitude. If you are doing this with the hope of impressing others with your ability to 'connect with the other side' or through the messages that you bring, or to become famous or get rich, it is unlikely you will get very far. Mediumship is not a fast way to make money. Yes, there are famous mediums. And yes, you can make money through this ability if you have reached the stage where you are ready to give mediumship readings to the public and you shouldn't feel guilty about charging reasonable rates (for you have to pay your rent/mortgage and provide food for the family). But making money and becoming famous are not good motivations.

Your mediumship gift should be treated with respect and gratitude.

It can help to mix with other mediums/psychics who are surrounded by spirits of light to help you develop your mediumship. Seek out people who are loving, humble and sincere and stay clear of mediums/psychics who are out to feed their ego through their mediumship ability.

Have you expressed your desire to the Divine/Universe that you wish to be a medium? If not, do so now and let spirit know you are working on your mediumship. Express your heartfelt desire to develop your mediumship ability and ask for help and guidance from your Spirit Guides who will be working with you as you develop your skills.

To be a successful medium, you need to be motivated by a strong desire to serve, to bring comfort to others through bringing positive, loving messages from spirit. As a medium and through the evidence you can give through your messages, you will be proving there is no such thing as 'death'; our soul exists in a never-ending cycle of regeneration, and death is the end of a 'physical chapter' ··· the spirit and soul live on.

Meditation is always an important part of any kind of psychic work and if possible, try to meditate even for five minutes every day. This helps you make a stronger connection with your Higher Self and in mediumship, it will be your Higher Self that will link with spirit.

Over the weeks ahead, as you make your way through this Workshop/Workbook, you will be introduced to information and exercises to help you work on your inner self and learn how to sense your energy and your guides' energy, all of which will help prepare you for when you start working on your mediumship ability.

Student responses:

- *I will leave this decision in the hands of our Creator and if it is meant to be then it will be; if not then that's absolutely OK with me too.* (Tutor: A beautifully humble approach.)
- *Lovely words of encouragement. I only wish to help people and bring comfort and if the angels wish this for me, it will be lovely.*
- *I'm happy when I can make a good connection with spirit for loved ones here, bringing proof that spirit are still around for them, that love never stops and spirit are happy once more.*
- *I have always wanted to help people. From the time I was a child I always wanted to know why things were happening with spirits that I never understood. Now I'm older my guides are helping me along the way and I know I'm meant to do this.*

Mediumship is the ability to sense and communicate with Spirit. Spirit applies to all beings who live on the other side, including our guides and angels. Some people are born with this ability and it comes naturally to them. Others work hard to develop their mediumship ability.

When Spirits communicate with us, they often give us symbols and it can help for you to study symbolism. Communication can be subtle, quiet and not always easy to interpret and the more we practice, the more we are able to distinguish between messages that come from spirit and our own conscious thoughts. It takes time to learn how to decipher the messages so we can pass them on to the sitter but this practice can be highly rewarding.

Practising meditation is important to help us connect with our higher self and the spirit world. Meditation is an altered state of conscious: a different state of awareness that deviates from our normal waking state such as day dreaming, sleep dreaming and hypnosis. Altered states of consciousness can happen naturally though we often don't recognise this. For instance if you become so engrossed in a task or activity such as painting, embroidery, craftwork, reading, gardening or video games that you lose track of time, you are in an altered state of awareness. When developing mediumship, you will take your meditations deeper to bring your Spirit Guides and angels closer.

When developing mediumship, it can also be useful to work on yourself: your fear and what may block your mediumship ability, how to raise your vibration and how to develop your psychic senses. There will be exercises in this Workbook to help in this respect.

Importance of Grounding, Shielding and Protection

Before doing any mediumship or psychic work it is important to ground shield, and protect. This should be a routine that is automatically and regularly carried out. Also, as you begin on this new journey, you might express your intent: state your desire to develop your mediumship skills for the highest good and ask for assistance from your guides and angels.

We all have an energy field that surrounds our body and everyone has a different vibration. This can change throughout the day, depending on our moods, experiences we encounter, our health or the stage of life we are going through.

Our energy field, which consists of many layers, can extend in all directions from a few inches to several feet. Each layer reflects our emotions, mind, mood, spirituality and overall health.

Throughout the day, we also encounter the energy within the environment. Having other people's energy enter our space can affect us too. We might pick up on their moodiness, negativity, excitement, joy. We might pick up their worries, fears or negative emotions and all of this can make us feel tired, drained and even physically ill.

When you are doing any kind of psychic work or if you are an empath, you are more likely to absorb the energy around you or the energy of the person you are reading for. However, there are easy ways to shield and protect yourself from this. For instance, make it a habit every day, even several times a day, to ground and shield yourself. It will get easier and easier to do this and to trust that your guides are working with you too so that with experience, you can do this within seconds.

How to Ground:

The first stage of protecting yourself from outside energy vibrations is to perform a grounding meditation. What does it mean, to ground yourself? In grounding yourself, you are restoring your connection with the earth. All it takes is a moment of silence and quietude to focus on yourself and your core.

One way to ground is to sit or stand with both feet on the ground and the palms of your hands facing upward. Take a few deep breaths and focus on your breathing to help calm your mind. Now imagine your body is a tree trunk and with each breath you exhale, visualise the roots of your tree travelling deeply into the soil, through the earth, down and down to the earth's core. Continue to breathe deeply. Now visualise your roots wrapping themselves securely around a huge crystal or rock.

Next, feel the earth's energy coming up through your roots and filling your being.

You are now grounded. Practice this regularly at any time standing or sitting and if possible, barefoot outside.

Note: If you are not grounded, you might feel dizzy, spaced out, clumsy or forgetful. I will give other methods on how to ground yourself later in this workbook.

Spiritual Cleansing

Once you have grounded yourself, you need to cleanse your energy field. To do this, imagine your body being surrounded by a coloured light. Choose a colour that you feel drawn to. Visualise this as being your aura. Spend a few minutes in silence, focusing on your breathing. Now try to imagine your aura and how far away from your body it extends. – It doesn't matter if you can't sense this, just 'knowing' it is there is enough and we will be doing exercises to help you feel your aura, later.

So, as you sit in silence, try to visualise your aura and look for energy that does not belong to you ··· that you have picked up, externally. You might assign a colour to outside energy, for instance dark grey. It might look like dark storm clouds covering an area. This helps you distinguish external energy from your own. Once you have sensed this foreign energy, visualise a shower of white cleansing light coming from above, washing over your aura and through your body and visualise the grey sludge of negative energy being wiped away, dropping off you and being washed away, into the core of the earth.

See these grey clouds or blotches falling away from you, dropping down into the earth and hold this intention until you feel all negative energy is removed.

Spiritual Shielding

Now you are grounded and you have cleansed your energy field, the final step is to protect yourself from absorbing energy from other people, places and the atmosphere around you. This final stage protects you from absorbing other people's anger, resentment, anxiety, sadness, fears, ill intentions and physical pain.

Visualising yourself within a crystal can be useful when you are working with people on a psychic level. Imagine a crystal that is big enough for you to go inside. The inside of this crystal is clear, healing and filled with loving light. The outside is mirrored, the mirrors facing outward so that negative energy is reflected back to where it came from and only positive energy can get through to you. Starting well above your head, all the way round you and down into the ground, visualise yourself standing inside this protective crystal. You feel relaxed and protected. Negative energy cannot penetrate your psychic barrier. Set the intention that it fall down into the earth and is cleansed or is sent back to its Source.

Another way to protect yourself is to visualise a protective white, blue or purple bubble surrounding your body and aura. Imagine it surrounding you completely and know that this is protecting you. Set the intention that your protective bubble will not let any harmful energy into your aura and it's as simple as that.

You might call upon your Spirit Guides to help you apply your protective bubble by saying "I call upon my highest and most loving guides to be with me to assist in protecting me from any negative energy."

Thank your guides for their help.

With practice, you will be able to ground and cleanse your energy field in less than five minutes.

Cleansing Meditation

Here's a Cleansing Meditation that can help relax you and prepare you for any kind of psychic work:

Find somewhere to relax.

Take a few deep breaths all the way into your stomach. Focus on your breathing.

Now imagine you are in the middle of a forest where all you can hear are the leaves on the trees stirring in the gentle breeze, birds singing and animals scurrying in the undergrowth. See yourself following a well-trodden path until you reach a small clearing.

Ahead of you is a deep pool. Water is flowing into the pool from a high waterfall. There are large rocks and stones at the edge of the pool. Imagine yourself walking towards the pool and sitting on one of the large stones. Take a look around you. Opposite there are trees, tall and strong, their branches heavy with leaves of all colours and sizes. You can hear them flutter like the sound of running water. Feel the breeze on your face: cool and gentle. Feel splashes of water from the waterfall as the water cascades into the pool.

Feel yourself relax. Now imagine a huge magnet slowly going down through your body from head to toe and attracting all the negativity within you: the frustrations of your daily life, uncertainties, anxieties; the upsets with other people and worries about the future ⋯ imagine these as gathering together like iron filings and being attracted to and sticking on to the magnet. Don't worry if you can't see this happening, just the intention is enough. This may be a little unpleasant but allow the magnet to reach your toes and leave your body taking with it all your negativity.

Now imagine this magnet being thrown into the pool and let it settle to the bottom, taking all your negative thoughts, feelings and worries with it. Here the water will cleanse the magnet and wash away all the negativity.

You are ready to stand up and walk towards the base of the waterfall. As you get close, the spray on your face feels stronger, cool and refreshing.

This waterfall is pure energy coming directly from the Divine. As you walk under the waterfall, feel yourself being cleansed by this pure white, clean energy. Feel the water wash over you from the top of your head to the tips of your toes. Feel this powerful stream of energy flowing all over and around you.

Now step away from the waterfall and onto a high rock. Stand with your face directed up towards the sky. Close your eyes in your visualisation and feel the healing energy of the Sun on your face. This bright pure white energy is filled with love and healing. Allow this energy to flow into the top of your head through the crown chakra, energising this chakra. Hold the energy there for a few moments and allow it to purify your connection to the universe.

Now feel the Sun's energy flowing into your third eye chakra. Hold this pure white light here for a moment and allow it to cleanse your intuitive ability and your psyche.

Move the energy down further to the throat chakra and allow it to cleanse this area to aid communication with the world around you and with spirit.

We're going to take this pure white energy down further now to your heart chakra. Allow it to thoroughly cleanse this area and feel yourself becoming more relaxed. Enjoy this tranquillity for a moment; note the awareness of being connected to all things seen and invisible.

Feel the energy flowing down further into and through your solar plexus chakra (between your navel and breast bone) cleansing, purifying and strengthening your spiritual and physical self. Feel your personal power and energy expanding.

Take the energy down through your sacral chakra now (navel and lower abdomen). Hold it there for a few moments, cleansing before allowing it to flow down to your root chakra (base of spine) before it flows down your legs and out through your feet, bringing a strong sense of foundation and anchoring within your physical body.

Step down from your rock now and prepare to return to your normal life. As you do, remember that your waterfall is always there whenever you feel a need to cleanse and energise. The energy from the waterfall and the Sun, high above in the sky, is Divine, Universal energy that flows through us all and bonds us all.

Whenever you want to, you can close your eyes and see yourself standing under the cleansing, purifying energy of the waterfall. Whenever you desire, step under your waterfall. The more you do this, the easier it will be for you to be there in an instant and it will cleanse your mind, body and spirit completely, leaving you feeling you have a strong and lasting connection to the Divine, to the collective unconscious, the universal consciousness that is the Source of all life and holds all things together.

Homework

As you begin to prepare yourself for mediumship and open yourself to mediumship, there are a few things you can do over the next few days. Please start a mediumship/psychic journal if you haven't already done so. Keep notes of your mediumship experiences, of intuitive/psychic impressions and messages you get. If, as you begin to develop your mediumship, you get a thought, vision, message that seems to come out of nowhere, make a note of it (don't forget to date your entries) and you could well realise at a later date why you got this message. For instance, you might suddenly see an image of someone pushing a pram, then a friend contacts you a few days later, to give you the good news that she is pregnant. I give this as an example of something that happened to me but at the same time, 'predicting pregnancy' is not something we advise or feel is ethical, for many reasons which will be discussed. It will be up to you on how you feel about passing on such information. I did not pass on this vision but accepted it as my guides' way of giving me evidence that I trust the visions that come to me.

Psychic and spirit messages often seem to come into your mind from out of nowhere ⋯ something that just suddenly jumps into your mind that has no bearing on your day's experiences or thoughts. In your journal, keep a note of your psychic exercises, dreams and mediumship experiences.

To receive messages from spirit, you need to open up to spirit. This can be a bit scary and I will be giving you guidance on how to deal with your fears and anxieties. Trust you have mediumship ability. We are all psychic and we can open ourselves up to mediumship. The biggest challenge is to get through the blockages that often come through us being conditioned to close or ignore that part of our self. I will help you, in this workbook, to open up to mediumship again.

So today, at this moment, I would like you to send a message to spirit to let them know you are open to spirit communication. Start by saying "I am a medium and I wish to communicate with spirit." Say this three times. You aren't yet asking for a message. You are, through doing this, letting spirit know you are preparing yourself to become a medium.

Over the days ahead, please slowly work through this book and try the exercises in each section for these will help you prepare yourself to receive messages from spirit.

Preparing for Mediumship 2 – Dealing with Fears and Anxieties

To open yourself to mediumship, you need to clear your mind of fears, negative thinking, expectations and worries. It can also help to face up to hang-ups from the past that you are conscious of or that you have blocked.

It might be that a childhood psychic experience now makes you nervous about opening up for mediumship. For instance, I accept myself as being psychic but I didn't want to acknowledge I have mediumship abilities. Yet because I have been teaching people to develop psychically and I always say practice, practice, practice and try things you've not done before too, to lead by example I tried mediumship.

Feedback was positive but I kept maintaining I would not do mediumship. Somehow I found the opportunities just coming to me and knew my guides were nudging me in this direction until I took a course on mediumship. At this same time, I started to remember experiences I had as a child where I could hear spirit voices. I always knew when this was coming, I didn't know what it was, only that it was from a place outside myself and my physical environment and I tried so hard to ignore it as it terrified me. For a long time they wouldn't go away. It took ages for me to learn how to control this until it stopped and then I forgot all about it. This is what's called 'shutting off your abilities'.

As I started on the mediumship course, I began to remember these experiences. I realised the doors were starting to open back up again but this time I would be the one in control. I have more experience now. I have worked in the psychic field all my adult life and started to realise that for much of it I have tried to suppress my mediumship ability.

I have now learned I can step through the door and develop my mediumship with safety and without fear.

We have many different fears and some may relate to mediumship. To help you confront these, you might remind yourself that spirits are just ordinary people like you or I with their own personalities who once had a family, job, hobbies and friends. And just as we can talk to each other in person, on the phone, on-line and even through body language, there are different ways in which we can communicate with spirit too.

Many mediums are empaths: they pick up other people's feelings, emotions and vibrations from the environment around them. When doing mediumship you might pick up the emotions of the person you are reading for, or the spirit around you. – Being able to connect with their loved ones can be as exciting for Spirit as it is for the sitter, who is comforted in the knowledge that their passed loved ones are still with them.

You can decide what you see, don't see, hear and don't hear. In other words you are the one who is in control. You can set boundaries as I will be explaining later.

Ways to Cope with Fear and Anxiety

Fear is something we have learned ⋯ something ⋯ an experience, imagination, belief or observation has taught us to be fearful. If you feel scared of opening up to mediumship, although it isn't easy to break out of this mind-set, there are ways to help alleviate your fears.

Affirmations can help. You might tell yourself for instance that 'everything WILL be okay' ⋯ repeat this ten times. Ask your guides, Guardian Angels, higher self or whatever you believe in to lead you in directions that are helpful to you. Put your trust in them and feel the fear melt away.

If you feel down, fearful, uncertain, worried or depressed or when your trust in your guides and the universe is low, you might try the following meditation.

Take a few deep breaths. Breathe in and out slowly and feel yourself start to relax.

Now with each breath you inhale, imagine you are inhaling a bright white light full of trust, love and security. Feel that light go deep down into your stomach. See the light go all through your body and all the way down to your toes.

Next, as you exhale, see all the fear, uncertainty and negativity that is within you being expelled out of your body. Then visualise yourself inhaling trust, love and light again.

Keep doing this until you feel the energy within start to shift as you draw in more light and love, expel doubts and fears, and renew your connection with your higher self.

Affirmation for Mediumship:

"I am love. I am peace. I am a medium. When I do mediumship I will trust that my Spirit Guides will help connect me with spirits that radiate love and truth. I will only see, hear and feel things that make me feel comfortable and safe. I will pass on messages that will bring comfort to the sitter. My guides will keep me safe at all times."

Sensing Spirit and Spirit Visitors

Scenarios most commonly described by students:

- I sometimes sense someone in my room or see people or animals out of the corner of my eyes and then when I turn they are gone.
- Sometimes when I'm in bed and have been falling asleep I feel someone sit on my bed. Or when watching TV, a book will fall or there's a noise in the room.
- Objects in my house get moved and aren't in the place I leave them. How can I tell whether the spirits I sense are evil or not?"

I have found that, especially when seeing movement out of the corner of my eye, or little flashes around me, this is spirit trying to get my attention. This used to happen to me a lot until I started on a mediumship course and began to accept my mediumship ability and then it got less and less.

When developing mediumship, fear is a very real part of the learning process for many of us. It certainly was for me, but I learned to trust in the good, in the light and in love and I always ground, cleanse and protect. Above all, I trust in the love and light and feel too that when we work in love and in raising our vibration, we attract spirit of a similar or higher vibration which can be very beautiful.

My daughter has regularly experienced objects being moved, going missing and then turning up later. This happened so often that her husband started to acknowledge and accept it was spirit. Her friends also actually witnessed an object flying across the living room floor. Once my daughter accepted her ability to see and sense spirit, this happened less. She is very aware of them around her now but she talks to them and has more control.

Prayer can be a big help when developing mediumship. Prayer can help you feel protected and gives you the control over negative feelings that initially might come in when you are first becoming aware of your mediumship ability.

I look upon Archangel Michael as my protector and if I am uneasy about anything I call upon him to wrap his cloak around me. I do feel that when people have experiences such as described in the above question, they are being given a little nudge to realise their potential.

Remember to ground, cleanse and protect regularly.

Think positive. Look to love and light. If spirit bothers you then please do be firm and ask them to stop because you aren't happy for them to be in your room when you are in bed, or in other places you wish to be your own territory.

Try not to think of this as a negative experience, as a lot of the time we can spook ourselves when there really is no need.

Remember too that negativity breeds negativity. Positivity breeds positivity. Likewise with love and light. The more light you bring in, the stronger it will be. Tell yourself there is no place for anything other than what you desire within your heart and soul.

Student Response

This feels like you were describing me! My brother had an unhappy spirit in his flat and this spirit disturbed his family on several occasions, I asked my guides/angels to help stop this situation and it worked! Many years ago I was woken every night with several things occurring, I was so tired and politely ask for it to stop and it did.

This student trusted his intuition and sensed how to deal with the situation in a positive and calm way. This also shows how the medium can and should always have control. This experience, for him, was confirmation of how he, as a medium, can take control of a situation, gently but firmly.

Preparing for Mediumship 3 – Sitting in the Power and Cutting Ties

Before you can recognise the different energies around you, you have to get to know what your own energy feels like. Sitting in the Power ··· also known as Sitting in Silence, will help you do this. It might feel as if you aren't doing anything but this is an important exercise to help you understand energy and build your psychic energy. Once you are familiar with how your own aura/energy feels, you will be able to know straight away when spirit or outside energy enters your aura, either visiting or if someone is probing your energy.

Try to do this exercise a few times a week. Even once a week will be beneficial. Ground and shield and ask your guides to step back so you can become aware of your energy but ask, too, that they still watch over you while you are doing this exercise. (Once you start to become aware of your energy, you can ask your guide to step back in and notice the difference in the energy around you). – We are all body, spirit and soul. Our conscious mind is our 'aware' mind, our 'analytical' mind, controlling our waking decisions and actions. Our subconscious holds our dreams, deepest desires and memories. Our subconscious mind is subjective and through our subconscious mind we reach our intuition and Higher Self.

Our body is the 'container', our vehicle in which resides our mind, soul and spirit. In the physical world, we carry out daily tasks, exercise, feed our body and focus on earthly matters. Meanwhile we are going through a spiritual journey and are connected, through our spirit within, to the spirit world, the Divine, the Source. Imagine a rainstorm. Each individual drop of rain coming down from the sky. Yet each drop is from the same Source and will return there in one form or another. Our spirit, too, will return to its Source to which it is eternally connected.

Sitting in the Power involves relaxing your body and clearing your mind to allow you to spend time within the Power, building your own energy, attuning yourself to your energy and blending with the Power of the Divine. As you relax, you take your mind within to find your spark of divinity. This is a bright light inside of you: the power of your soul. As you Sit-in-the-Power, you move towards this light to merge and blend with the light of your soul. Sitting in the Power is not about connecting with Spirit, your Guides or your Angels. It is all about being with the energy and expanding your soul. It can be a very beautiful experience.

There are many variations of Sitting in the Power and you can experiment to find the one that works for you.
Here is a one that I practice regularly:
Firstly, set the intent that you are about to sit in the power. Relax and prepare yourself as you would do for meditation.
Cleanse your energy and call on Archangel Michael to cut all negative cords that are around you. – I will introduce you to Archangel Michael again, later.

Once sitting comfortably, imagine you are breathing in through your solar plexus and exhaling out through this same area. Take slow, deep, relaxing breaths.

As you breathe in and out, focusing on your solar plexus, feel the power of your energy gradually grow. Feel your energy fill you and visualise it expanding outwards.

Feel the power of your energy. The more you do this, the more you will recognise your energy ⋯ it might feel lively, calm, electrical or excited ⋯ this will depend on your own experience. Mine is a very calm energy.

You are now Sitting in the Power. Sit for a while and get used to the feeling.

Another method of Sitting in the Power is again to cleanse, cut cords and protect.

Sit with your feet firmly on the ground. Close your eyes and 'feel' your feet firmly fixed to the earth. See your roots, deep below the surface and attach them to a large crystal.

Now turn your attention to your Heart Chakra (heart area). Visualise a bright white light in your Heart Chakra.

Now take your attention to your Crown Chakra and visualise divine, white, healing light flowing down into your crown, filling the whole of the upper half of your body.

Return your focus on your feet and your roots and visualise energy coming up from deep within the earth, up through your roots, through your body to meet the white light in your heart area.

Visualise the energy from above and from below mixing, combining and filling your whole being.

Now visualise the combined energy extending from your body for about three feet or whatever makes you feel comfortable.

You are now Sitting in the Power. You are filling your body and your aura with this powerful energy.

Sit, relaxed, in this state, breathing easily.

If you can't visualise the energy, that's okay. Just reading the above words and setting the intention is enough for it to be happening.

Relax now and enjoy this quiet time, Sitting in the Power.

Homework

For this Homework, I would like you to try this exercise in Feeling the Energy.

We all feel energy differently: some people just sense it, some feel it with their body – they might get a tingling sensation, for instance. Some hear, some taste and some can smell subtle energies. As you work on your psychic development you will discover more about how you perceive energy. No one way is any better than others.

This next exercise will help increase your awareness of subtle energies.

Relax and allow your mind to quieten.

Take a few deep breaths as this helps you relax.

Now rub the palms of your hands together briskly for about 15 seconds.

Hold your hands in front of you, palms facing each other. Slowly bring your palms toward each other and then away again, like you are playing an accordion.

Can you feel the difference in energy as your palms move closer and move away from each other? Notice any sensations you feel in your hands and fingers.

You might fee a thick sensation between your palms. You might feel tingling, warmth, pulsing or other sensations. If this is the first time you've felt subtle energy it can be quite amazing.

Now you are going to boost this energy between your palms.

Close your eyes and ask your Spirit Guides to work with you. Ask that they help make you sensitive to all subtle energies around you. Ask that they help amplify your sensitivity to subtle energy and thank them for their help.

Next hold your palms in front of you as before. Can you feel a difference? Does the energy feel stronger now? – Have fun.

Through carrying out this exercise regularly, you are creating a stronger bond between your conscious mind, body and spirit. You will become more sensitive to your own energy and more aware of subtle changes in your energy as you pick up the different energies from around you. This increasing sensitivity will help you sense those in the spirit world as they work with us and connections made become stronger and clearer and easier for us to detect.

Cutting Ties

You have learned how to ground, shield and cleanse and I now want to introduce you to the need to cut ties. When we go about our daily routines, as mentioned above, we can pick up other people's energy and the energy in the environment and this can get attached to our aura. In addition to this, our thoughts can connect us with people as their thoughts, feelings and wishes can attach to our aura.

If someone is thinking of us in a positive, loving way, this is good but if they might be resentful of us or wish us harm, then this is negative energy being aimed at and coming into our aura. We can protect ourselves from this through regularly shielding as in the routines already given.

We can also cut ties. Cutting ties is letting go of psychic/emotional ties attached to us from people we meet and situations we experience. Others who are attached to you might be feeding from your lines. This is why we might sometimes feel drained when in some people's company. They are feeding off your energy. It is not always a bad thing to have ties to others but when we have too much negativity around us, this can leave us fatigued. We need to let go of any negative energy around us and by cutting this negative energy away, we are making room for new.

To cut ties, relax and take a few deep breaths. Take your mind to your Heart Chakra and visualise the cords from your heart attached to all people and situations around you. Some of these will be loving. Some will feel murky and negative. Know that the loving ones will always remain. Visualise a large pair of scissors cutting through all the negative ties. This can be one by one, or as one fell swoop. As you cut ties, you are letting go of all this emotional burden you have been carrying around.

Once ties are cut, imagine unconditional love, as a pure white, healing light, being sent to all those you have cut ties from.

Another way to cut ties is to ask Archangel Michael, a Warrior of Light, to use his amazing Sword of Light to help us break away from all negative beliefs, behaviours, relationships or circumstances.

It's not difficult to call on the angels. You don't need any magical ritual and you don't need to have strong powers of visualisation. Just say their name and they will be there. Archangel Michael offers protection and helps boost your courage and confidence. When you're feeling vulnerable, He is the Angel to call on for help. As you call His name, imagine yourself being surrounded by a glowing, blue healing light.

For help with clearing your aura and cutting negative ties, ask aloud or silently:

"Archangel Michael, please cut away and vacuum any negative energies, toxins and cords from my mind, body, spirit and aura." Close your eyes and imagine Archangel Michael's blue light surrounding you and see Him slicing gently through negative ties with his blue sword. Enjoy the pleasant feelings of Michael clearing you. Once you feel lighter and grounded, ask Archangel Michael to surround you with white pure light of love and to protect you from lower energies you may come into contact with in the future.

Don't forget to thank the angels when you work with them.

Preparing for Mediumship 4 –An Introduction to the 'Clairs'

We all have different types of psychic abilities and can receive messages and psychic information in different ways. Understanding this can help you realise how you pick things up psychically and how you've probably already been doing this without noticing. Also, how to develop your natural psychic abilities.

The different types of psychic abilities are classified within a group of 'clairs' ··· each has a name beginning with 'clair' which is French for 'clear'.

There is a correlation between the clairs and our five senses (sight, hearing, taste, feeling and touch) and some of us will use more than one clair in our psychic and mediumship work.

Here's a brief explanation of the main clairs:

Clairvoyance (clear-seeing): Clairvoyance includes seeing visions (moving or static) in our minds with eyes that are open or closed. These are mental images and some describe them as being like a video that is being played in their mind. Images can also come like a flash into your head. Clairvoyance includes vivid dreams, seeing colours, auras, energy fields around humans, plants and animals. We receive these psychic impressions through our Third Eye in the centre of our forehead.

Claircognizance (clear-knowing): Claircognizance is clear knowing or psychic-knowing. You just 'know' something is right even though you may have no facts or evidence to back up this knowledge. When pieces of information just randomly pop into your head that seem to come from nowhere (nothing you've seen, heard or thought about recently) this is clairgognizance. You may for instance 'know' why someone has phoned or messaged you before they've uttered a word. You might know about a place, event or person and yet have no idea how you just 'know'. We receive these psychic impressions through our Crown Chakra which is located at the top of our head.

Clairaudience (clear-hearing): Clairaudience means clear-hearing. Messages can come to you through the words of a song, for instance if you had something on your mind and you hear words in a song that seem to speak directly to you. You might hear your name being called when there is no one else in the room. Hearing voices within ··· this might seem like someone else's voice or you just hear words inside your head that come from nowhere or from outside. You might hear conversations though there are no others in a room. A clairaudient experience I had was during a Weekend Psychic Development workshop at a Roman Fort. The energy there was amazing and while lying in bed trying to sleep, I suddenly was aware of conversations going on. I could hear many different voices, young people and old and different accents. I could hear them distinctly and was fascinated as I knew this was not coming from my physical environment and I was wide awake. I was 'aware' of these voices for a long time and stayed very still, listening, trying to work out and remember what was being said. My other experience of Clairaudience was when I was younger as I mentioned before, when I could hear voices, whispers, noises that couldn't be explained and which I eventually managed to push away and block for a very long time.

These voices, music and sounds we hear can be spirit or even echoes of the past. We receive these messages from either side of our head, just above our ears.

Clairsentience (clear-feeling or clear-sensing):

Clairsentience means clear-feeling or clear-sensing and this tends to be one of the psychic abilities we are first to notice and find easiest to develop. You may have called this your 'intuition' ⋯ times when you sensed energies coming from the environment, other people, animals or coming from nowhere that you can distinguish but you just 'sense' they are there. When we are sensing or feeling things about our environment or other people we couldn't possibly have already known, we are using our clairsentience ability. This may come to you as a gut-feeling, a queasy feeling that warns you something isn't right or a bad feeling about a situation. It may even be a good feeling about a decision. We receive these psychic impressions through our solar plexus.

Clairalience (clear-smelling): Have you ever sat in a room to smell floral fragrances, baking, food or a cigar, for instance, yet knowing there was nothing around that could be causing these odours? Clairalience is smelling odours that have no physical Source. This can occur when spirit is around (for instance smelling your late aunt's favourite perfume) and it can be spirits way of letting us know they are near. Smells are often associated with haunted areas.

Clairambience (clear-tasting): Clairambiance occurs when we might taste flavours of food without having eaten them.

If you really wish to develop your mediumship ability, you will be willing to work on it. We might look on mediumship as a 'gift' as art is a gift, musical talent is a gift, writing poetry even is a gift and like all gifts, the more we practice and the more we work to develop them, the stronger they get. Here are some exercises to help you develop your 'clairs':

Visualisation exercises help you develop your Clairvoyance (clear-seeing)

I want to mention Visualisation now as when we do psychic work we often rely on our ability to visualise in order to receive and give messages. We also use our psychic visualisation in grounding, cleansing and protection techniques. Not everyone finds it easy to visualise images and when this occurs, just setting the intention or saying the words is enough. Good visualization will help a lot when meditating and when you are giving readings and this is a skill that can be improved with practice.

Visualisation is linked with imagination and creativity. This is why creative work helps enhance our intuition. Visualisation is the ability to 'see' people, objects and places in the mind's eye. Imagination is a form of visualisation. When we dream, we are using our powers of visualisation.

Visualisation can be helpful in emotional and physical healing. Or, in order to attract opportunities that might help us realise our goals, we might focus our imagination on experiences we would like to happen in our lives in the future, repeating these visualisations, using all our senses (sight, sound, smell and touch). This technique is based on the idea that visualising positive happenings can change emotions (helps relax us, calm us and enhances hope) and relaxes the body. Many psychologists believe that visualisation is a powerful tool for change.

Visualisation can help you overcome fears and anxiety, calm your mind, ease tension, lower your blood pressure and achieve helpful insights.

As mentioned above, mediums and psychics can receive information in many different ways (feelings, visions, an 'inner knowing', smells and/or hearing). Information can be received by any of the senses. By developing your ability to visualise, you will be better able to receive visual information that can help you when giving mediumistic and psychic readings.

Visualisation Exercise 1: Try this relaxing meditation:

Make yourself comfortable and relax.
Close your eyes.
Imagine you are standing on the edge of a lake. There is a rowing boat at the shore beside you.
There is someone waiting to row you to the other side of the lake.
Step into the boat and sit down opposite this person.
Relax as the boat leaves the shore.
Feel the steady rhythm of the oars as they glide through the water.
Feel the boat gently rocking in the water.
As the boat moves towards the middle of the lake, take this chance to look around. What do you see? What do you hear? What do you smell?
What is your companion wearing? Do they have a face? Do they remind you of anyone?
Now see the boat edging closer to the shore.
As it reaches the shore, step out of the boat and thank your companion for this calming experience.
As you step out of the boat, notice where you are. Is the other side of the lake any different to your starting point? Are there any people/animals here waiting to meet you? Spend as long as you like looking around until you find a place to sit and relax, then open your eyes.

Make notes of your impressions in your Psychic journal.

Visualisation Exercise 2: For this exercise you need to sit in a darkened room in front of a lighted candle.
Look at the flame. Keep your eyes focused on the flame for a few minutes.

New close your eyes and hold the image of the flame in your head for as long as you can.

Keep repeating this exercise until you can hold an image of the flame in your mind's eye without having to sit in front of the candle.

Visualisation Exercise 3: Close your eyes and imagine you are looking at the blank page of a large book. Firstly start by visualising numbers on this page. Start with the number 1. Fill the page with the number 1. Focus on this for a few seconds then imagine turning the page and seeing the number 2 on the next blank page. Keep doing this until you work up to the number 10. As a variation to this exercise you might use letters or objects.

Exercises to help you develop Clairaudience

Next we move on to exercises that help you develop your Clairaudience. You might find that Clairaudience is one of your main 'clairs' and it will come naturally to you to develop this ability. You may 'hear' sounds outside your normal senses occasionally but it could take many years to develop clairaudience so like all psychic abilities, practice helps a lot. – Your Throat Chakra is associated with Clairaudience. You might find blue gemstones help especially Lapis Lazuli. Archangel Michael is also associated with the Throat Chakra and the development of Clairaudience. You might ask that Archangel Michael help you through this prayer: "Archangel Michael, I ask that you help me develop my Clairaudience. I ask that you protect me by only allowing sounds of love and light that are for my Highest Good and for the Highest Good of those I come into contact with. I thank you for helping me develop this gift."

Clairaudience Exercise 1: 'Listen' ⋯ with your ears, simply listen to every noise around you. Close your eyes and take note of every sound you can hear. The television in the room next door, birds chirping, leaves blowing in the wind, cars passing on the road outside, the hum of the washing machine ⋯ differentiate all the sounds you can hear and write them down in your journal.

Clairaudience Exercise 2: Listen to classical music. As you are listening, can you differentiate each instrument in the orchestra? Can you hear the violins, pianos, drums, flutes, cello etc.? Again this exercise helps you focus on your hearing and different sounds.

Clairaudience Exercise 3: 'Imagine' ⋯Close your eyes and imagine a piece of music being played. Can you hear each instrument? Does it sound real? Listen to your favourite song in your head. Imagine a friend or loved one is talking to you. Can you 'hear' their voice? Imagine different scenarios ⋯ a busy town centre: can you hear the traffic on the road, people calling each other, doors closing or other activity? ⋯ Practice this for a few minutes each day.

Clairaudience Exercise 4: 'Imagine' ⋯ Relax. Place your protection bubble around you. Now imagine a radio in your mind. See yourself switching on the radio. Next, visualise yourself turning the dial as you would a radio to tune into the station. Relax and allow yourself to listen to the sounds ⋯ you might hear a lot of buzzing, you might hear blurred words or indistinct music. Keep trying this exercise and you may receive clearer sounds and messages with practice.

Clairaudience Exercise 5: 'Meditate' ⋯ Meditation is essential in developing all psychic abilities.

Finally, have fun

Here is another simple exercise to help you develop your Clairs:

Relax and close your eyes. Take in a few deep breaths to help calm your mind.

Now start to imagine a piece of fruit ⋯ an orange, apple or banana for instance.

Next focus on the fruit. Keep your mind on the orange (or whatever you have chosen) and don't allow other thoughts to intrude. Your focus is purely on the fruit. Imagine yourself looking at the orange from all sides. You can see its skin and its colour. You can see it from the right side or left side. From the top and from the bottom. Observe it carefully. Does its skin have a pattern? Is it rough or smooth? Does it have one colour or more? You are now focusing on the details.

Next imagine yourself peeling the orange (or whichever fruit chosen). Can you smell the fruit? Pop a slice into your mouth (in your imagination). Can you taste it? Repeat this exercise a few times to help train your focus and your imagination. You can also try visualising different objects every time you do this exercise.

Developing Mediumship

As you become more aware of your psychic/mediumship ability you might 'feel' spirit around you, hear voices or notice smells that cannot be explained. You might see sparkles in the corner of your eyes or shadows in your peripheral vision. Your peripheral vision is that part of your vision that occurs outside the centre of your gaze. If you hold a pen at arm's length in front of you, this is your main focus, the area that is in sharpest focus and outside of this, is less focused. Yet the peripheral vision is surprisingly sophisticated, drawing our attention to things outside the main focus of our gaze.

Your peripheral vision picks up on subtle changes in energy that our main gaze might miss. Mediums are often become aware of shifts in energy through their peripheral vision.

For this exercise, you get to play with your peripheral vision. Today, when you are out and about, try using your peripheral vision to notice what is 'outside' your main gaze. For instance if you are walking through town, use your peripheral vision to especially notice what's going on in the buildings or on the street around you.

In your mind, try to focus on what you are seeing out of the corners of your eyes, paying attention too, to any feelings that this brings to you, then stop and return down the street and focus your gaze on what you saw in your peripheral vision to 'see' how this relates to what you were picking up. Were there any specific colours that drew your attention, any shapes, patterns, shadows? Any feelings relating to this exercise can give you clues on how your day might go, how your relationships might be today, patterns in your life. For instance, if something that caught your eye gave you a sense of excitement, it may be that in the next few hours, an experience, meeting or person will uplift you.

Write down your impressions in your journal and as you become more aware of your ability to notice these different signs and patterns, how what you see out of the corner of your eyes can relate to your emotions/feelings ··· this will help you interpret your intuitive impressions.

Student Response
"I constantly see and sense 'someone' standing in the doorway of my office and I look up and they are gone. Sometimes I've had to get up and check that there is no one there or someone wasn't really out there waiting for me. Yesterday, it was a real 'busy' day in this respect and I feel that I have had to hear these words, just for confirmation."

Signs come in many ways and this was confirmation for this student that she was sensing spirit.

Preparing for Mediumship 5 –Learn to Love Yourself

As a medium, you will be sharing love and passing on loving messages from spirit. To 'feel' the love, you need also to learn to love yourself.

Love yourself ⋯

Before you love another you need to love yourself.

Don't be so critical of yourself.
Don't think there is nothing to love about yourself.
Just because other people criticise you it doesn't mean they are right
Don't feel guilty about doing the things you love
Don't worry about what other people might think
Release other people's opinions

Thoughts only have power over us if we allow this.
Dismiss negative thoughts as meaningless
Choose to think thoughts that nourish your soul

Keep telling yourself everyday:

I love myself
I approve of myself
I let go of thought patterns that keep me stuck in the past
I value myself
I am happy and strong

Talk to yourself like you would to someone you love

Homework

Spend some time alone (switch off our mobile phone, turn off your laptop). Just be with yourself. You might stay indoors or go out for a walk but what's important is that you just be with 'you' and start feeling comfortable being who you are.

Preparing for Mediumship 6 – Calming your Mind and Emotions and Knowing your Mind

Calming the mind and emotions helps in all psychic work. It can be hard to tune into your Higher Self if you are feeling fretful, angry, jealous, irritable or excited. In mediumship, you are inviting spirit to communicate through you, to pass on messages to your sitter.

Our daily life can be stressful and situations we go through every day can trigger a mix of emotions, both positive and negative. As you prepare to do any kind of psychic work or mediumship, it is good to spend a wee while quietening and calming your mind and your emotions. Remember that your emotional outlook can influence your spiritual connection. Your emotions and your thoughts are your own and can be controlled by you.

Allow yourself to accept and acknowledge thoughts and emotions. If some feel overwhelming or painful, it might help to analyse and ask why you are feeling this way as this will help a better connection between your mind and emotions. There is a lot of information online on how you might balance mind, body and spirit if you feel this might help you face up to and release fear, anxiety, anger or upset. Forgiveness, acceptance or changing the way you look at a situation can sometimes help restore emotional equilibrium.

Meditation to Clear your Mind

When working as a medium, you need to prepare your mind so it becomes, in effect, an 'empty vessel' in order for you to receive and pass on messages from spirit.

As you clear your mind, you aren't trying to forcefully push out thoughts as this could have the opposite effect. Instead, imagine your thoughts are like leaves blowing in the wind. Acknowledge them and let them blow on past.

Close your eyes and take three slow, deep breaths, focusing on your breathing.

Keep focusing on your breathing and feel your mind and body relaxing.

If thoughts come into your mind, acknowledge them, then let them go like those leaves blowing in the wind and return your focus on your breathing.

The more you do this meditation, the more quickly you will notice all the mental clutter clearing and your mind becoming still. Eventually, you will find you can reach this meditative state quite naturally, quickly and effortlessly.

When your mind is empty of thought, you are ready for a mediumship/psychic session.

Student Response

Oh I love this since my head is so FULL!!

Tutor Reply: for mediumship I was taught we had to make ourselves an 'empty vessel' ⋯ I'm not sure I feel comfortable totally with that implication but I do feel that we have to empty our mind to allow us to receive and pass on messages and know the thoughts aren't our own. The more we meditate like this and clear our minds, the more we get to know our own mind. I hope that makes sense.

Student: *Yes that makes total sense but with the activity and shifting changes within my family day to day I sometimes have a hard time. When I have time I am going to lock myself in a room with a hotel sign that reads "Do not disturb!" Nah! I love my family ⋯ but I could do with clearing my mind, sometimes!*

Homework – Observing Energy

Observe your family, partner, children, friends, colleagues, neighbours. Can you see how they move in and out of each other's energy fields?
Think about what it is that draws you close to certain people
Think about what it is that makes you want to pull away from others.

Student Response

As I was trying to re-read this week's Homework, my computer screen kept moving up and down, just enough to blur the words ⋯ interesting as I can instantly tell when certain family members are around me as I feel their energy

Tutor: It is good to be able to feel other people's energy and spirit's energy and distinguish it from your own.

Know your own Mind

Why is it important to know your own mind when developing mediumship? Through meditation and calming your mind you start to recognise those thoughts that will creep into your mind and as you meditate you should not fight these thoughts but acknowledge them and send them on their way. These are your thoughts. As you begin mediumship and psychic work, you will start to recognise those images, flashes of information, thoughts, feelings and sounds that come to you or into your mind from out of nowhere and will intuitively know these to be messages from spirit.

In knowing your own mind, you can analyse your way of thinking. Are your thoughts fearful, anxious or negative? Do memories that cause you to feel angry, upset or badly done to, keep coming into your mind? Or do you strive to think positively, to feel the love around you, to show love and compassion to yourself and to the world? If your mind is overshadowed with negative thinking, strive to change negative thoughts with something more hopeful and positive. Strive to balance your mind for as you develop your mediumship, keeping your mind in balance will help you recognise the images/messages you get that are coming from the spirit world.

Also, if you feel negatively about yourself, you might feel negatively about the world in general and working on yourself, learning to love yourself, will help you spread the love which is a big motivation for most mediums.

Homework

In your Journal, start a new page with the heading: How do I feel about myself at this present time? Now just write, without thinking about it. Go with the flow and enjoy this exercise in analysing your thoughts.

Preparing for Mediumship 7 – How to Raise your Vibration and Simple Techniques to Communicate with your Spirit Guides

Everyone has a different vibration and we have been doing exercises to sense your own and other people's energy. Our vibration is like our personal energy signature. Imagine switching on a radio and tuning into a station. Sometimes the signal is strong and clear, sometimes it is weak and you can 'just' pick up what's being said or other times it is plain frustrating and all you can do is distinguish you have picked up a signal but can't tune into it properly at all. Your vibration will influence your experiences, relationships and situations you go through and equally all of these will influence your vibration.

So, if you encounter people who make you feel wary or who just aren't your cup of tea, it's likely you're both at a different vibrational frequency. This does not mean either of you or any better than the other, just that you aren't of the same wave-length and that's okay: there are plenty others who will share your wave-length and plenty others who will share theirs. If you find yourself feeling drained in someone's company, it could be that they are at a lower vibrational frequency and are feeding-off your higher vibrational energy. If you keep encountering negative, hostile or upsetting situations, these are low vibrational energy experiences and this can drain your energy, or it could be due to you engaging in lower vibrational energy patterns.

We live in a challenging world and it would be impossible to be at a high energy vibration constantly but there are ways of recognising when your vibration is low and ways, too, to raise your vibration.

WHAT MIGHT LOWER YOUR VIBRATION

Toxic environments
Toxic relationships
Negative thoughts
Anger
Jealousy
Resentment
White sugar
Contentious environment
Constant arguing
Clinging on to the past
Too much alcohol
Worry
Anxiety
Burning the candle at both ends

I'm sure you can think of more!

TIPS ON HOW TO RAISE YOUR VIBRATION

Here are some ways to raise your energy vibration:
Love
Grounding
Laughter
Smile
Creativity and passion
Walking in nature or on the beach

Working/spending time in the garden
Breathe deeply and focus on breathing
Meditation
Yoga
Love
Classical Music
Meditation Music
Eating leafy greens, raisins, watermelons, greens, almonds, dandelion, beetroot
Sunshine
Relaxation
Activities with children
Acceptance
Volunteer work
Helping others
Counting your blessings
Kindness
Forgiveness
Joy
Burn lavender oil
Love – you just can't give or receive too much love!

An Introduction to Spirit Guides

We still have a little bit more to talk about on preparation before you start to communicate with spirit but I'd like to now introduce you to some simple techniques to communicate with your Spirit Guides and your loved ones in spirit.

Before trying to bring messages from spirit to other people, it can help to quietly try to communicate with friends and loved ones, in spirit. You might do this through asking spirit to come to you in a dream, asking for a sign from a loved one in spirit or ask your guides to answer a question while you sleep. Do this, as you are falling asleep and when you wake up, try to remember your dreams or what is the first thing that comes into your mind as you wake.

Or you could meditate on a question for your Spirit Guides.

Other ways to increase your sensitivity to spirit is to try to communicate with spirit while in the hypnagogic state (that transitional state between wakefulness and sleeping), stream of consciousness writing (ask your Spirit Guide for a message from spirit then just write without stopping. If your brain freezes up then just write the same word over and over until something comes to you. Don't 'think' about what you are writing and don't worry about punctuation, just write).

Raise your vibration through tuning into universal love for remember, the higher your vibration, the easier it will be for spirit to communicate with you. Approach mediumship in a loving, positive frame of mind. – Remember that communication is a two-way process. When we use the telephone, we don't just listen, we take an active part in the conversation. When you start to communicate with spirit, join in with the conversation. Ask them questions (out loud or in your mind) and listen for answers.

Dream Visitors

When you dream of loved ones in spirit, you might wonder whether it is 'just a dream', or was this really a visit from spirit? Spirit often visit us in our dreams and these dreams differ from ordinary dreams because they are so vivid and because they feel so real. When waking from such a dream, you might feel as if it really happened, like remembering a memory. You might recall details of the dream vividly. You may have 'felt' the embrace of a loved one during your dream and it felt so real, as if they were really there with you.

When communicating with spirit, don't forget your protection bubble, ground yourself, then ask your guides to come close. Then calm your mind into a meditative state. Now imagine yourself picking up a telephone and calling a loved one in the name of Love, using their name and see yourself dialing their birth-date. If you feel you cannot connect in a mediation, ask that they visit you in a dream.

Write down any spirit communication experience in your journal.

Revision

Soon we will be starting on mediumship exercises. You will no doubt have worked out that before starting on mediumship, the focus has been on preparing yourself to be a medium. You should now know how to ground, cleanse and shield to protect yourself when doing psychic work and indeed, when out and about. You should be Sitting- in-the-Power regularly as this helps you build your own power, recognise your own energy and raise your vibrational energy so that Spirit can communicate their messages through you. Meditation helps calm your mind and also it is through getting into a meditative state that your mediumship will unfold. Meditation will also help you recognise your own thought patterns and thoughts to enable you to distinguish your own thoughts to messages that come in from outside (in mediumship, from spirit). As a medium, it is important that you get into the habit of protecting your aura on a daily basis. This isn't difficult. It isn't time consuming. It can be done at any time and eventually you will find you can do it naturally and instantly.

When you are working with spirit, you are more susceptible to picking up negative energy, but don't let the word 'negative' worry you. As you work on yourself, you are building love, compassion, creativity and forgiveness within. As you work on these aspects of your nature, your light grows stronger and will attract similar energy vibrations your way.

Work in love and you will attract love. Even so, cleanse and protect regularly just like when we go out in the garden and get our hands dirty, we will wash them. Every experience attracts different energy our way from the people around us, the environment and spirit and cleansing our aura should be as natural as washing our hands.

Homework

Experiment with different ways to ground and protect yourself to find a one you feel comfortable with. Here are a few:

Waterfall: I love this one best: Imagine you are standing in a waterfall and the water is cleansing all negativity from your body, washing it into the stream below and taking it to the sea where it will be transformed into positive energy.

Shower: When you stand in the shower visualise all negative energy flowing from your body, from your aura and draining away with the water.

Protection Bubble: Imagine a white, blue or purple protective light coming down from the Divine, flowing over your head, round your body and under your feet. You are surrounded by this protective bubble and protected from any negative energy coming into your aura.

Carry a piece of black tourmaline with you: This is a great crystal for protection against any negative energy and helps ground you too.

Smudge your aura: Smudging is a Native American practice that uses white sage to cleanse any negative energy.

Hug a Tree: Grounding yourself prevents you from having that 'floating', 'not being with it', dizzy feeling. You can use visualisation to ground, you can hug a tree, walk barefoot in the garden. Hold a stone or pebble. Wash the dishes, tidy the house, weed the garden, do something that connects you with the earth and everyday life.

Use sound to clear your aura: Some tones can clear our energy. You might use a drum, tuning fork, handheld chime or Tibetan singing bowl to cleanse your aura.

Preparing for Mediumship 8 – You are the One in Charge

Remember when doing mediumship that you are in control and you are in charge. Establishing boundaries is important from the start.

When you begin to develop as a medium you will be a magnet for spirit. But just imagine, you don't leave the door of your home unlocked for anyone to come in at any time day or night. Spirit will try to get your attention whatever you are doing ⋯ cooking, cleaning, bathing ⋯ so just as we lock our doors and enjoy private time in our homes by ourselves, spirit must respect it too when we lock our spiritual door.

So how do you set the rules and remain in charge? Decide on your mediumship working hours and let your guides and spirit know this. If for instance you have children and need to focus on your family during the day, or your job, let spirit know that when you are otherwise engaged, your door is closed to them. If you don't want to set specific hours a day for mediumship, imagine yourself in your meeting place (see spirit meeting-place meditation) and see a door to this meeting place being closed with an open/closed sign hanging on the door. When the sign says closed, let spirit know that you mean it. When you are in this place, the sign can say 'open'. Or you might imagine this place with a light switch and when you enter, switch the light on to let spirit know they are welcome to join you. Switch it off as you leave to show you 'aren't in' for mediumship.

If spirit does show up outside your open-hours, remind them you are closed and ask them to leave. Refuse to acknowledge them. Keep doing this and they will get the message.

Setting Boundaries when Linking with Spirit

Now you know how to open and close when doing mediumship, what boundaries do you want to set during the mediumship session? You can work with your guides for this too. Let them know what's off limits and what kind of behaviour you expect when doing your readings. Are you for instance ready to 'feel' or 'hear' spirit but not ready to 'see' them yet? Can they touch you? Can they talk to you? Decide on what is and what's not allowed and ask your guides to help ensure spirit respect this too.

Spirit, like us, might get excited like a child at Christmas when they find someone they can link with to pass their messages on. Spirit come to us at a higher vibration that can be very fast anyway and if it seems like images, feelings and messages are coming to you at such a fast rate you can't get a hold of them, ask spirit to slow down so you can understand.

Remember to set the rules: you are the one in charge

Homework

It is important in so many ways that you know that in mediumship, you are the one in control. Can you think of areas in which you need to be in control in your mediumship and why?

Part 2 – Working with Spirit

Working with Spirit 1 – Connecting with your Spirit Guides

When you are linking with spirit you will also be working with your Spirit Guide/s. Your Spirit Guide will help protect you and will be there for you any time you need them. Even if you can't feel your Spirit Guide around you, simply asking that they come close and setting the intention is enough to bring them into your aura. Just send out the thought and they will respond.

As you work on your mediumship, it is reassuring to know your guides are close to you. As you get to know your Spirit Guide, you will start to recognise their individual sign to let you know they are near. They will use this same sign many times and this will help you learn to recognise it. Some people call this sign their guide's calling card.

To help this process along, take a moment now to sit down quietly. Take a few deep breaths. Relax and let go of all your fears and doubts as you exhale.

Now ask one of your main Spirit Guides to come close to you, to say 'hello'. Sit quietly and wait. Do you feel a subtle change in the energy around you? (If you have been doing the Sitting in the Power exercise you will be familiar with your own energy).

So, let go of your doubts, relax and ask your guide to show you a sign that they are close. People experience this in different ways. Some go hot; some go cold. You might feel shivers down your spine or down your arms. Your eyelids might flicker, your lips might tingle or you could feel a gentle breeze at the side of your face.

Once you have been given this sign, this is your guide's calling card and they will show this to you every time you work with spirit as a sign that your guide is there, protecting you.

If you don't get anything, don't worry. Over the days ahead you might notice the same thing happening again and again. This is your guide helping you find your confirmation sign ⋯ their calling card. Some people will get it straight away. For others it can take a wee while.

So, relax and open up to receive your Spirit Guide's calling card. Once you have it, make a note of it in your journal.

How to Communicate with your Spirit Guides

Your Spirit Guides help guide you through life. Some are with you from birth to the end, some will come to you during those phases in your life when you may need help with a specific purpose. All will help you fulfil your soul's purpose.

Every one of us can communicate with our Spirit Guides and our Guardian Angels. We can talk to them out loud or in our minds, just as if we are talking to a friend who is sitting next to us, and please trust that they will hear. We can all receive messages from our Spirit Guides. These can be subtle, but if you watch for them and become more aware of them, you will start to 'know' signs that they are near.

Spirit Guides, as their name suggests, help 'guide' us through our life but they won't ever force us to do anything. We will receive their assistance through intuitive feelings, sudden thoughts that come into our mind, flashes of inspiration or seeming coincidences. We can all receive the help of our guides but some people who may be set in their ways or thinking, oblivious to their intuitive feelings or adamant that they aren't spiritual, might choose to ignore it, which of course, is their prerogative.

Some people will naturally follow the guidance of their Spirit Guides without realising they are doing so. They may act on an idea or inspiration without recognising this as coming from outside themselves. However, it is possible to learn to recognise signs, messages and communications from your Spirit Guides and to improve your receptivity to spirit.

For this exercise, you need pen and paper. Start with the intention of writing about an important issue in your life or an important question you have for your Spirit Guide. You might even ask about your mediumship and spirituality.

Begin as always, by grounding and placing your protective bubble around you, then ask your Guardian Angels to watch over you, protect you and guide you.

Now relax and start writing. Just write and write for about twenty minutes. Don't think about what you are writing. Don't stop to wonder about spelling or punctuation. Just write. If you suddenly stop, write the same word over and over until the flow starts up again. As you write, try to keep your mind in a meditative state. Just get the words down as they come to you. It may come in sentences, in one word ideas or in a conversation form. – Just write.

Try to do this every day. It may seem stilted and may not come easily at first but over time, you could be amazed by the results. Thank your guides after the exercise and then read through, edit and add (with the date) to your journal.

Connecting with your Spirit Guides

You are likely to have a number of Spirit Guides with different names and different purposes. They will help you with anything in your life if you ask for their help. A Spirit Guide has been through and learned from all the earthly lessons that must be learned. They are there to assist and guide you through your own chosen path. They will never make choices or decisions for you ⋯ you have your own freewill ⋯ but they will guide and advise especially if you wish for this.

It can help to learn the name of your guides or choose a name for them, especially if this is all new to you. This can make you feel like you are developing a relationship with them.

There are a number of ways you can link with your guides/Guardian Angels and these include:

- Talking to them silently in your mind. Whatever you want to say to them, just say it and they will always listen. Talk out loud if you prefer. Imagine they're sitting next to you and open up a conversation with your guides.
- Write down your thoughts and feelings in a diary or journal. Or sketch, doodle or draw them. Through expressing your thoughts in words or creatively, you are helping to make your guides aware of the issues that are on your mind.
- Write poetry.
- Write a letter addressed to your guides or Guardian Angels. ⋯ Don't edit what you write ⋯ as with the exercise we have just completed, just let the words flow and let them come to you. It could be that as you're writing you will find yourself veering off in directions you hadn't thought of or you will be writing words that hadn't come to you before. This is your guides' way of helping to answer your questions.
- Trust your intuition. Your hunches and gut instinct can be messages from your guides or Guardian Angels.
- Meditate regularly ⋯ there are many ways to meditate. When you find your mind going in on itself while washing dishes or walking for instance, this is a form of meditation. Other ways to

meditate are to focus on your breathing, clear your mind of thoughts and relax. Music can be very relaxing and can help you feel connected with your Higher Self.

• Be sensitive to signs that your guides and angels are talking to you ⋯ some people see feathers and coins. You might hear a song that is meaningful to you when you need to hear it or hear words in a conversation that answer a question that has been on your mind.

These are simple, initial ways to link with your guides and Guardian Angels. You might also try guided meditations to help you connect and form a stronger relationship with these divine beings.

Working with Spirit 2 – Opening yourself up for Mediumship

To open ourselves up to mediumship we need to do all we can to free our mind from thoughts, expectations and blockages. We need to be clear and open to 'receive' messages and for this we have to control thoughts that are going on in our head. For in order to be a 'medium' – to convey a message from one place to be heard in another – we need our minds to be as quiet as possible, to be able to receive the messages.

As a medium, we receive messages from spirit to pass on to our sitter. ⋯ In this though I have to say that although our minds need to be clear in order to receive messages, we still retain the power to think about how the messages we convey might affect the sitter. We can and should only pass on information we deem is for their Highest Good. You should never pass on messages that go against your conscience.

Everyone is unique and every medium will have their own way to make that connection with the spirit world. Psychic information can also come to mediums in a number of different ways, as you learned in Part 1 of this Workbook.

As you open yourself up, you will be a magnet for spirit. This is why, as you begin, you need to know that you are the one in charge here. Not spirit. It is 'you' who will determine and decide when you invite those beyond the veil, to come to you. When your door is closed, those in spirit need to respect this. Your guides will help you here, along with some visualisation exercises that I will give you.

Remember to keep up with your mediumship journal ⋯ make a note of your meditations and your readings and about how you feel and how you are progressing.

Messages received from the spirit world by mediums come through their Higher Self with the help of their Spirit Guides and Guardian Angels. The medium (you) will serve as a link between our world and the higher realms.

As you learned in Part 1 of this Workbook, an important first step in mediumship is to send a message to your guides that you would like to work with spirit. ⋯ Think about how you want to work as a medium. Let your guides be aware of your boundaries. I will not for instance touch on how a person may have died as I just can't deal with that at the present moment. Many mediums will use this as evidence and it is good evidence. I can only cope with getting a feel for the personality of a person's loved ones' on the other side and hope to pick up memories or information that can be used as evidence. I do not want to 'see' spirit ⋯ I 'feel' ⋯ and I ask my guides to intervene should ever I might not be comfortable with information received. So they are in effect standing guard at the door and only letting information through that I feel comfortable with.

To open ourselves up to mediumship we need to clear our minds of thought and analysis with respect to wondering 'what does this mean?'; 'Where has it come from?'; 'Is this just my imagination?' The moment we start to question, we might lose the connection.

You will also need to clear your mind of worries, everyday thoughts, fears and anxieties. (See Preparing for Mediumship 2). Guilt, regret and the inability to forgive (yourself or others) can cause blockages in your energy which may eventually manifest physically. If, for instance, painful memories intrude on your thoughts, this can bring on physical and emotional reactions. When you dwell on past mistakes, this can trigger negative emotions such as jealousy, anger or shame and this can lower your vibration.

It isn't unusual to have blockages to overcome so don't feel you are any different to other mediums. When we start developing our spiritual side, an important lesson is the need to heal from the past. This helps us reduce energetic blockages and raise our vibration, which as you now already know, is needed for conscious spirit communication.

So, a good proportion of blockages will tend to depend on us healing from the past as this is where these blockages began to accumulate. You might ask your Spirit Guides to help you in this healing. You may also find that Reiki can help remove energy blockages.

Another obstacle can be a lack of dedication or willingness to put in time, effort, dedication and the patience mediumship requires. Like all skills worth developing, your mediumship ability will build at a pace that is comfortable for you if you are willing to dedicate yourself to this. Remember, there is no quick way to make 'mediumship happen' and there is nothing to fear about communicating with spirits.

Leave your ego outside. Ego has no place in mediumship. Your purpose is to help people and to bring them comfort through passing on the messages you receive from their loved ones in spirit. You have no need for ego-boosting praise. Any feedback received is purely to help you in your development. Being grateful to those in the spirit world, and to your guides for helping you pass on this information is good for your soul. Have a grateful heart.

Homework - Quietening the Mind and Ego

When your mind is filled with thoughts, plans, fears and anxieties, this robs you of peace and with all this mental chatter going on in your head, it can often be hard to hear your inner-voice, your intuition. When you are giving readings and become fearful that you might get it wrong, or start questioning your ability, this is your conscious mind interfering with your intuition and when you do start to question, you can make wrong choices, looking back later and wishing you had gone with your initial feelings.

There are a number of ways to quieten your mind to encourage you to trust your Higher Self and for your Homework, here are just a few to choose from:

- Write poetry ⋯ get all that is going on inside out on paper. This can be therapeutic. Alternatively, doodle, draw a picture ordo some art. Then instead of having a scattered mind, your thoughts will become more focused.
- Meditate regularly ⋯ meditation will help bring you inner stillness.

- Take a gentle walk: take in your surroundings and allow your mind to relax. Gentle exercise can help your mind feel calm too.
- Let go of negative attachments and let go of negative expectations. Try to go for a whole day without allowing your mind to become attached to 'outcomes'. Stay in the present.
- Cuddle up with your pet ···stroking your cat or dog will help relax you too.
- Detox your body: Avoid addictive substances such as alcohol, coffee, cigarettes and other drugs. If you've had feelings that it is time for a detox, then this is a good time to start. Drink plenty water. Eat plenty fruit and veg and try herbal tea.
- Call upon the Angels to help you in your spiritual work. Archangel Raphael, the Angel of Healing, is always ready to support you in your release of chemicals. Ask AA Raphael to please help release you of your cravings for ··· (fill in the blank). Confirm that you are ready to release these cravings, now and forever.
- Archangel Jophiel is the Angel to call upon to help encourage positive, loving thoughts. This is the Archangel who will support you in releasing your doubts and fears and any ego-based energies. AA Jophiel can also help you clear the clutter of your mind and your environment. Surround yourself with soft lighting, crystals, pleasant fragrances and beautiful music. When you need a little spiritual uplift, call upon Archangel Jophiel.
- Before going to sleep, call on Archangel Michael (Angel of Protection) and ask that He comes to your dreams to help clear away any fears and anxieties so you are able to develop your

mediumship ability and move forward with your Soul's Purpose.

You might now feel ready to send a message to the spirit world that you would like to communicate with them. Remember to introduce yourself to spirit and thank them for coming to you as this can help strengthen the connection.

Working with Spirit 3 – Your Mediumship Stone or Crystal

There are a number of gemstones and crystals that can be used to enhance your mediumship ability but I was taught to find a special mediumship stone and I would like to share this with you as you might find it helpful as you start on your mediumship journey.

To find a mediumship stone, you could go for a walk in a park or in the countryside or by the sea. Or it may just be a stone that you see in your garden. When you see a stone you feel drawn to, hold it in your hands. Imagine yourself connecting with the stone. Does it feel as if you might be able to work with the energy of this stone?

You might also choose a favourite crystal or gemstone to be your mediumship stone.

Once you feel you have found your mediumship stone, whenever you meditate and prepare yourself for mediumship, hold it in the palm of your hands. The energy between you and your mediumship stone will start to build.

Meditate to feel a connection with your stone. Try to use your psychic senses to feel as if you merge with the stone. Visualise the energy in the stone flickering alight within it and expanding outward until it surrounds the stone and merges with your hands.

Next program the stone by saying that you want to connect with its energy while you are opening yourself for mediumship and for this energy to aid your focus on mediumship. You can also program your stone and its energy to protect you while you are doing mediumship.

It is then important only to pick up the stone/crystal when you are opening up for mediumship. If you carry it around with you, or keep it under your pillow, you will be open all the time and this can drain you.

So as you do your readings you might find that holding your stone helps you to focus and connect easier with spirit. I have a special malachite wolf crystal that was gifted to me by a friend that I hold when giving readings.

Important: Remember your mediumship stone will open you up for mediumship. You should have a special place to keep it when not doing mediumship work. It isn't good to carry this stone with you all of the time otherwise this will keep you open to spirit. Use it for mediumship then once you have closed down, put your stone away too.

Student Response:

Oh Carole Anne, I was away for a weekend and the hotel we stayed at had a bay with a little beach behind it. We stopped to just go look at the water before we were to drive home and I saw this (to me) very unusual rock and brought it home with me, just anticipating what my special connection was going to be with it. It has sat on my desk at home for a few weeks now and after learning about this, I just looked at my stone and smiled. I picked it up and on the back of it, I see my initials and I am just elated! The front, when I look at it, I see an image of a blonde girl which was what attracted me to it in the first place. I am so happy right now!

Tutor: It's as if you found this in anticipation of this workshop or your guides were smiling as you found it, knowing exactly what you would be using it for. Last night, when I was meditating, I saw a young girl and thought of you. I wonder if this was linked too. I'm so happy you have found a purpose for your rock.

Student: *I had such a strong feeling when I found it. I love this so much.*

Tutor: Maybe a sign too that now is a good time to work on your mediumship. It is something that is very natural to you and strong within you ⋯ all you need is to trust in this. I feel that good foundations to work on are the lessons you have learned so far about grounding, cleansing and shielding and the only way you can go from here is up, up and away. I'm excited for you as I can see your huge mediumship potential ⋯ stronger than mine; so much stronger. ⋯ It is a pleasure to be able to help nudge you in the right direction and I know it's going to be wonderful to watch your mediumship grow.

Student: *I get so excited when connections are made. I am so glad you encouraged me to do this class even though I wasn't sure at the time. It seems spirit is finding me time!*

Student 2: *I have just found my stone and was drawn to it instantly for mediumship. Thank you.*

Working with Spirit 4 – Your Spirit Meeting Place, Opening and Closing and Tools for Mediumship

It can help, when doing mediumship, to have a special place in your mind to meet spirits and Spirit Guides. Especially when beginning mediumship, this can make you feel safe and protected.

To do this, find a place where you can be comfortable and relax.

Take a few deep breaths and feel all your worries and negative thoughts and emotions drain away.

Now imagine yourself on a long country road. This road can lead to anywhere. Start walking. Feel yourself in this place. Feel the road beneath your feet. See the sky above you. Notice the clouds. There are birds flying in the sky. Now turn your attention back to the road.

It is changing and taking you to a special place. This might be a little country cottage, a castle, a walled garden, a beach cove or a tree house, even. – Somewhere you will always feel safe and comfortable. Enter this place and take a look around you. Familiarise yourself with the room/garden/area. You will come here often.

Find a seat and sit down and close your eyes (within your meditation). Ask your Spirit Guide/Guardian Angel to come to you.

Now open your eyes in your meditation and see or feel someone sitting with you. You feel safe. You feel loved. You feel protected. Let them know that this is the place you will be meeting regularly in the future. This is where you can ask for guidance, converse with your guides, and with those in the spirit world, even, if this is what you desire.

Ask your Spirit Guide to only allow loving, truthful spirits to converse with you. Ask that the messages they bring should only be for your good and for the highest good of those you are reading for. Ask that they protect you from any experience that will make you fearful or uncomfortable.

Now take a few moments to calm your mind again. Feel the comforting presence of your Spirit Guide/Guardian Angel. When you feel ready, ask for a symbol you can use when you are opening yourself to mediumship. This might be a light switch that you can switch on when you are open for mediumship and off when you are closed. Or you might see a door that again you can open when you are doing mediumship work and close afterwards. The aim of this is so that you can open and close for mediumship and you don't leave yourself open for spirit to visit you anytime and anywhere, as has already been mentioned. Your mediumship stone can also be used for this purpose. The sign is 'your' sign and individual to you.

Now you know your sign, agree with your guides that you will use this whenever you do mediumship, so you are all in agreement over when you are and aren't open for spirit.

Take a few more moments with your guides, thank them for being with you and for their guidance before opening your eyes and returning to your everyday world.

Energy Awareness

One way of enhancing your medium ability is to tune into the energy field surrounding other people. Over the next few days start trying to differentiate your own energy and other people's energy. To tune into energy fields you need to engage your psychic senses. Use your eyes, your feelings and your intuition and give yourself time and space to tune into the different vibrations that are around you. Notice how you intuitively respond to people and how they react to you and note this in your Journal.

Sensing Energy

Try to sense other people's energy fields.
You don't have to 'see' the energy literally. You might sense a colour around them. What colours, shapes and density do you 'sense' is their aura. Are there any patterns apparent?

Note how people's energy changes depending on their mood. – When someone is happy, what energy are you sensing? When someone is sad, notice the difference.

Sensing other people's energy is a good way to start tuning into your own psychic senses.

Students Response

Student 1: *I see white around people.*

Tutor 1: You are seeing their aura. It can be any colour. I'm just starting to see a thin line around people.

Student 1: *For me, it is only white in colour. No other colours yet but they will come eventually, I'm sure. Isn't it fascinating!*

Tutor 1: It is! The more I learn and do, the more it uplifts me. It gives me such joy when working for spirit in any way, especially giving readings of any kind.

Student 2: *I see the colour white around people.*

Student 3: *This is something I have not experienced yet. I do not see colours around people. – Maybe someday.*

Tutor 2: I can't 'see' auras as such either but what you might find is that you can 'feel' the colours. Instead of 'seeing' with our eyes, some people can sense the colours of auras or see them in their mind's eye. For this you might focus on a person while in a relaxed, meditative state and ask your guides to help you visualise their colours. You could be surprised by what you get.

Another Exercise for Energy Awareness

How do you recognise male or female energy? One way to practice on feeling male/female energy is next time you're in a queue and there's someone behind you, without looking, 'feel' with your energy. Ground and protect first (you can do this quickly as you get accustomed to this as a habit) then push your energy bubble out so it touches the person's energy behind you. Do they feel male or female?

Once you get an answer in your head, turn around and check, then visualise your energy drawing back into yourself as you do so.

This is similar to the way we work when someone in spirit draws close to us that we know isn't our Spirit Guide.

Tools for Mediumship

Especially when first developing mediumship, some mediums who are also psychic might find it helpful to make that first connection with the spirit world through using tools. Tools such as tarot, angel or oracle cards, crystal balls, runes or tea-leaves can act as a trigger that opens you mediumistically and brings forth spirit.

Ouija Boards and Séances

There are many tools that can help you develop your mediumship ability. Some can be helpful such as the ones just described, others are dangerous. Many people ask about Ouija Boards and Séances and I would advise strongly against these.

This is why: When using these tools or when taking part in a séance, you are inviting spirits in. You are asking that they come and talk to you but you have no control at all over the type of spirits that accept this invitation. It's like opening your door and inviting any passer-by to come into your home, without knowing where they are from, whether you can trust them or what motivation they may have to accept your invitation.

It is believed that there are different spiritual planes and there are many spirits that will stay close to the earth plane, waiting for the chance to be let in. Some are mischievous, malicious, angry and clever. Some will disguise themselves as being kind and helpful when their motivations are far from good. These lower spirits are masters of deception and can be clever in gaining your trust. Once you have invited these kind of spirits into your life and home, they can hang around and cause a lot of disruption and upheaval.

Steer clear of these kind of activities is my advice though you have your own freewill and can make your own choice regarding this.

My preference is to connect with spirit motivated by love and that come through for my highest good and the highest good of those I read for.

Student Response:

Student 2: *I am so glad you brought this up as I have never used the Ouija board before but something I can't explain – call it wisdom, intuition or guidance from the soul tells me to steer clear of them. It has always been my belief that this is a tool that is dark in its origins and I believe nothing from a place of love and light will come forth by this means of communication. I believe the dark forces prey on the ignorance or curiosity of those who use them. – Just my personal opinion of course and no offence intended.*

Tutor: I agree that it is something to steer clear of as you just don't know what you are 'letting in'. Some people will try this for fun, but it isn't fun and can be pretty dangerous for mental/spiritual and emotional health.

Student 2: *I agree. I would never mess around with Ouija Boards. I've heard so many 'not so nice' things about them and I think it is only inviting in unwanted spirits.*
Student 3: *I agree, there is something deep in me that says: stay clear of them', so I do.*
Student 4: *OMG, NEVER AN Ouija Board for me!*
Student 5: *Nooooo Ouija Boards! Bad stuff!*

Tutor: I'm so glad we all feel the same and this perspective also shows we take a serious and respectful view of mediumship and the spirit world. We can all form our own opinions and go with our own feelings but mine is that this isn't a game or something to be toyed with.

A little revision

This is a good time to pause and think about what we have learned so far. You now know what mediumship is, you have thought about what motivates you to develop your mediumship and you know how important it is to work on ways of increasing your receptivity to your Spirit Guides and to the spirit world. You have expressed your desire to the Universe of your wishes to connect with Spirit and know your Spirit Guides are helping you develop this ability.

You know that Spirit work at a higher vibrational level and you are aware of how to work on raising your vibration. Keeping your attitude positive, avoiding negative thoughts and words, and filling your being and your life with love, helps you maintain a high vibration. Drinking plenty water, a nutritious diet and getting the rest and exercise your body needs is also important in mediumship development.

You know the importance of uncluttering your mind so you can sense, feel or hear spirit more clearly. Meditation and working on your psychic development helps increase your receptivity to spirit. Spirit communication is often subtle and quiet and can be so very easy to miss if we aren't listening or paying attention.

Developing mediumship takes dedication, commitment and practice ⋯ lots of practice.

You know how to ground, cleanse and shield and why you need to do this. You will be Sitting-in-the-Power regularly. You have experimented with energy to help you know your own energy and how to recognise your Spirit Guide's Calling Card. You are aware of some different methods to communicate with spirits and your Spirit Guides and how to open and close. You are also aware of the importance of being able to deliver messages in a compassionate, caring and responsible manner.

Next we will be talking about how those in the spirit world communicate with us and how to decipher these messages.

Working with Spirit 5 – Spirit Communication

Contrary to what people might think, our loved ones on the other side don't just jump out in front of us, and chat with us, as easily as we talk to each other. If only it was that simple! Many, many people will have mediumistic ability but don't realise that spirits are trying to communicate with them because they aren't aware of, or haven't learned how to recognise the signs.

Our loved ones in the spirit world communicate in subtle ways. You might notice shivers down your spine, get goose-bumps or feel a whisper of a breeze against your cheek. You might notice a shift in energy or temperature when spirit is around you. You could hear a song on the radio that relates to something or someone you've been thinking about or that has special meaning for you. Have you ever found an item in a strange place and this made you think of a loved one in spirit? Or do you notice the same numbers appearing around you: on the clock, your mobile, car registration numbers etc.? Eventually you just can't keep brushing this off as coincidence. This is your Spirit Guides or loved ones in spirit, connecting with you in a way that you can notice and acknowledge.

When we connect with spirit, they communicate largely through symbols. They might also give us words that we recognise as coming into our head that are not our own thoughts.

You may be given smells, sounds, symbols and scenes. It can take time to learn how to decipher these messages and this is why practice really helps you develop your mediumship. Many Spirit messages can come through thoughts that just pop into your mind. You might for instance, be working on a project and a sudden idea on how you can improve your work will seem to come out of nowhere. This could be a loved one in spirit making a suggestion to you.

Symbols

When we communicate with Spirit, we firstly receive the information directly, in the form of a word, feeling or image that can be passed on to our sitter. Or we may receive a symbol which we need to interpret in order to relay spirit's message to our sitter. Their feedback helps give us confirmation that we have interpreted the symbol correctly.

So, sometimes we can pass on what we receive, as we receive it, for instance if we see or sense a person or personality and can describe this as it comes to us. Or if we hear a word that just enters our mind that we feel may be meaningful to the sitter. But other times we are given symbols and the actual message isn't always clear.

Just like in dreams, often what we 'see' in dreams are 'symbols' and we need to look behind the dream, to interpret the symbol in order to understand the dream meaning. Spirit sometimes use symbols to deliver messages and we may need to work out the meaning of the symbol to pass the message on to our sitter. This can be a little confusing at first until you get used to working with symbols.

Here's an example: if you are given a rose, what does this mean to you? It might, for you, be a symbol of love but for another person who maybe once fell off their bike and landed in a prickly rose bush and has ever since felt roses caused pain, this could be a warning of a thorny situation to come. In which case, the message you pass on will be very different.

It is important to interpret symbols through what they mean to 'you' as symbols can mean many different things to many different people depending on their life's experiences, and your Spirit Guide will be giving you symbols they know you will interpret your way.

Mediumship

Every medium will work in their own way and you might experiment with different ways of connecting with spirit until you find a method you feel comfortable with. I like to use the words 'feel comfortable' as this is so important in all aspects of psychic work.

If at any time, you feel uneasy, follow your conscience. As you are aware now, the first steps begin with working on yourself. You need to believe you have mediumship ability and you can connect with spirits. This can mean freeing your mind of doubts, fears and any disbelief so you might embrace your mediumship and let it flow.

Initially, when you start developing your mediumship, it could help to join a group of like-minded people who are also working towards the same goal. If you can join a development circle under the guidance of a qualified or experienced medium, this would be ideal but not everyone has access to a mediumship circle. You might find an online group focusing on psychic and mediumship development and again, trust how you feel about the group energy. If it doesn't feel right for you, find another one. This does not mean there is anything negative or wrong with the way some groups are run, but we all have different vibrations and if you aren't in tune with the energy of those within the group, it will always feel out of kilter for you.

We run a number of Facebook Groups including: "Spirit Guided Readings and Workshops – Free and Paid Psychic Readings" where we offer loving guidance and regular Workshops. That said, again, this is not saying you would find this the right one for you. Experiment with different groups, different people and different mediumship techniques. That's part of the fun of this wonderful journey.

You can also learn how to safely develop your mediumship through research, reading books such as this one, talking to, and watching other mediums, on-line courses and of course, practice. – The more you practice, the stronger your ability will grow.

We have already discussed techniques to open up to mediumship. You can follow these, grounding, shielding, holding your mediumship stone and meeting your guides and spirits in your special place or here are two more simple methods:

Method 1 - Mediumship

Ground and shield.

Spirit work at a higher frequency so as you prepare to give mediumship, you need to raise your vibration. Visualise a white light surrounding you. You will be working within this light and it should only be white. Ask your guides that they only allow spirit that resonate at your vibration or higher to be allowed close and that you are only told what is in your highest good and for the greatest good of those you are reading for.

Relax, close your eyes, and bring your focus to your heart chakra. Feel the love in your heart. Think of someone or something that makes your heart feel light and full of love. If you have a pet cat or dog, for instance, feel the love you have for your fur-baby. This is all about 'feeling'. Don't bring thoughts into it. The energy you are feeling is love for love is the highest vibrational frequency there is, and as you feel the love, your vibration will rise. You might also keep your vibration high by playing gentle music in the background that helps to relax you and keeps you feeling filled with love. Burn candles or incense and lower the lights so your room helps you become calm and relaxed.

Now imagine a waterfall in a breeze and the breeze is whipping up the water and blowing the spray up and away. This is like your love, radiating out to the universe. Those in the spirit world can feel your love, pick up on that love and will come to meet you. For now that you have raised your vibration, they will lower theirs so you are vibrating on the same level to enable you to feel, hear, see and sense the energy of friends and loved ones beyond the veil.

You are now working in the light and merging with the Universal Consciousness. Imagine you have entered a slip road to join a motorway. Carefully, you ease into the traffic and then you are going with the flow. You were on the outside, now you are in, going with the flow and picking up the speed to keep up pace. This is like the relationship you have with spirit and how you communicate. Your energy will merge with the Universal Consciousness, you are linked with the spirit world and now you can communicate.

Bringing your attention to your Third Eye Chakra, ask if there is a message from spirit. When you feel someone come through, talk to them in your mind, or out loud. Remember you need to be present and fully present. If there are a hundred thoughts going on in your head and you call spirit in, it isn't going to work.

Ask spirit to join you and ask them to give you a message or symbol that might be meaningful for your sitter. Allow all your senses to be alert to their messages. What do you feel, hear, sense, smell, see, taste? Ask specific questions such as: what was their age when they passed? What was their job? Were they married? Did they have a big family? You might set out to gain three pieces of evidential information – this is evidence to prove that you do have a connection with someone's loved one in spirit. Remember that spirit communicate through symbols. So for instance you might ask about their job and they show you their hands, rough and darkened with soil and you might get the instant impression they were a gardener. Trust that first feeling, thought or impression. Trust.

Once you feel the spirit energy lessen around you or as if it is not quite flowing – you will feel a difference in the energy – this suggests the conversation is over. Thank spirit for linking with you. Thank your guides for their help. Ground, cleanse and shield.

Method 2 – Mediumship

Cleanse, ground and visualise your protective bubble around you, over your head, round your body and under your feet. Visualise your aura filling this bubble. I always imagine this as being blue but you can choose any colour you want.

Now it is time to focus on your breathing and this will help calm you and clear your mind. Take a few deep breaths. Every time you breathe out, visualise your aura bubble expanding.

Next, imagine a beam of white, healing light beaming down from the skies and coming down into your crown chakra, just above your head. See this light filling your body. If you can't visualise your bubble or this white light, that's okay. Reading these words and setting the intention works just as well. – See this white light filling your aura bubble.

You should now feel calm and relaxed.

At this point ask your Spirit Guide to come to you and stand behind you in your aura bubble so you can feel them there. Your Spirit Guide knows you are ready to open to mediumship and you are inviting them to come close to you, to guide and protect you. You can ask this of them in your mind too.
Close your eyes and feel your Spirit Guide behind you. Wait until you see or feel their calling card.

Now you might ask spirit to come forward for the person you are reading for. Whatever comes into your mind ··· trust this. You might get words, see images, get feelings, smells or hear voices.

Pass on any message received to your sitter.

When you feel spirit leave you, thank them for coming forward. Thank your Spirit Guide for working with you and helping you connect. Thank them for their love and protection.

Now visualise the energy that has built up during the reading to drain down through your body to your roots and downward still, to seep into the earth. Imagine your aura bubble retracting back into your body.

Use your closing down image (this may be switching off a light or visualising yourself closing a door or putting up a 'closed' sign). Use whichever is your preferred way to close down and disconnect. Remember you need to do this after each mediumship session or you will have spirit visiting you at any time, night or day, which can be draining.

Cleanse and ground and you might say a small prayer ··· again, whatever feels right for you.

After psychic work, remember to drink plenty water.

Working with Spirit 6 – Evidential Mediumship

Mediumship is the ability to connect people in the physical world with their loved ones in spirit. Reading a 'person' based on their personal energy is a psychic reading and this is the difference between psychics and mediums. All mediums are psychic but not every psychic is a medium. Mediums connect with spirit and through this will bring information to their sitter that will provide them with undeniable evidence that their loved ones in spirit have moved on to a spiritual plane, but can still be with those they love in the physical world, when they choose to be so.

Mediums receive information from spirit differently; everyone is unique. They might be clairvoyant (see spirit with their mind's eye), clairaudient (using their inner-ear), they may get feelings or smells. Information will be received through their psychic senses at various degrees of strength. The way a medium gives information is important. Some will say they 'give what they get' without censoring and no matter how upsetting it might be. The people I work with and I, strongly disagree. We feel that as a medium/psychic we have a big responsibility to protect the emotional well-being of those we read for. Diverting slightly, but, you also have a responsibility to yourself and if while giving a reading you sense, feel or see anything that upsets you and you feel you don't want to continue, politely (without distressing your sitter) explain that spirit has left you and you can't get any more. End the reading. Ask spirit to leave and ask your Spirit Guide to clear your space, cleanse, ground and protect you.

Back to the reading and as you pass on information to your sitter, word it in a way that will cause them no upset or distress. Your aim should be to leave them feeling comforted and uplifted. As you receive information, try to give as much as possible of what you are getting.

I have just been to an 'evening of mediumship' and the medium gave six readings. Every one of these was basically the same with no evidence whatsoever. In each reading she said that spirit wanted to 'put their arms around the sitter'; in three of the readings, eye problems were given, two had problems with their feet and squashed toes; every one had their 'back' mentioned and they all had friends who 'used them in some way' (the medium's words). Thrown in for good measure was a grandmother, mother or father. She put on a great performance, but I feel that is all it was: a performance. I saw no evidence of mediumship.

Saying "I have grandmother on your dad's side and she is giving you her love", and leaving it at that provides the sitter with no evidence. Being more specific, for instance, saying "I feel a female energy with me and I'd like to give you more to see if you can recognise her. She seems to have a grandmother energy and I feel she could be on your father's side of the family. I see she is a tall, slim woman who loved to wear the colour green. She shows me an apron with flowers on which may have been one of her favourites. Her hair is short and curly. She shows me a garden full of vegetables and a man working in this garden which may have been your grandfather or your father. I sense she was an outgoing, friendly person who loved to gossip with her neighbours. She says she used to pick you up from school. Do you recognise this spirit?"

In this way you are giving 'evidential information' to confirm you have a firm connection.

When giving mediumship, sometimes names will come to you but this can be hard for mediums and if you can't get names, don't worry. Some spirit will give you information on their appearance or their personality for you to pass on. Some may give a memory or may even offer information that refers to the sitter's current circumstances as a way of showing they are with them. The information can be subtle and difficult to pick up at first but the more you practice the stronger your mediumship will become.

You may not always get a good connection; you may not always be one hundred per cent correct. No one is. If, during a reading, the sitter cannot understand what you are passing on, you might ask your Spirit Guide to help strengthen the connection. Some of the reasons the connection may be weak include:

- The sitter may be subconsciously blocking the link: if you feel this, help them relax and release tension by encouraging them to breathe deeply and calm their mind.
- It might be the first time a certain spirit has come through – It takes energy and practice for our loved ones on the other side to connect with us too.
- If you are reading within a large group of people, you may have picked up a message for a different person.
- Your Spirit Guides may be protecting you from making a connection that is not for your highest good.

We cannot dictate who comes through. So, if we are reading for someone, your sitter may hope to hear from a certain loved one in spirit but this may not always happen. Your main aim in mediumship is to be able to provide your sitter with validation and confirmation that their loved ones in spirit are still around them, but none of us can dictate who will come through.

Fun Exercise

As you develop your mediumship, you will be receiving messages (through words, images, symbols and smells etc.) from their loved ones in spirit to pass on to your sitter. This provides the sitter with evidence that their loved ones are still around.

Imagine you are on the other side and giving a medium a message for your loved ones. What symbols would you use? Words, memories, songs? – Think of how you would try to get a message across, to let a loved one know you are still with them and make them feel loved.

Student Response

Student 1: *I've just been talking to a medium friend on the phone. She has a lot of health problems and she said when she gets over to the spirit side, she'll certainly be having a word with them. We laughed and decided she would probably come back as a guide for people suffering health-wise as she has battled with health issues for so long. She also said that if she did, she wouldn't be sending fluffy feathers and gentle signs. She'd be giving 'in their face' signs to get medical help or get to the hospital. But she would make them laugh too!*

Student 2: *I would drop a tarot card in front of them as I always work with tarot and they will know for sure it is me as no one else in the family reads cards.*

Words and Mediumship

Words can't change reality but they can change how people perceive reality. Words can influence our perception more than we realise. For instance if you are told a new neighbour is meddlesome, you will be predisposed to think of this neighbour as being a trouble maker regardless of their actual personality. Having heard one single word to describe this neighbour creates a filter through which you will view this person and until you really get to know them, you might always have it in your mind that they can be 'meddlesome'.

Words have power and words can trigger feelings, emotions and reactions. Here, I am going to list some words. Sit for a moment and study each word. Say it over in your mind. How does the word make you 'feel'? This is to help you when you receive messages from spirit to pass it on to others, for as you understand your reaction to just one word, you might also sense the deeper associations that could be meaningful to your sitter.

Here's a list of words. Spend a little while on each one, sensing what each one triggers within you:

Angel
Dog
Horse
Blindfold
Blue blanket
Pink blanket
Ice
Keys

Swords
Hammer
Clouds
Moon
Rain
Tree
Ocean
Stars
Bird
Armour
Boat
Bridge
Heart

Student Response

Student 1: *This was really good for me. It made me centre myself and really think about each word and what it means to me.*

Student 2: *Wow, this is really interesting to think about ··· and so true what we can perceive from a single word and the feelings it evoked ··· loved this exercise.*

Exercise – What does it feel like, to communicate with those in spirit?

Words, visions, images and smells that are communicated by spirit are often experienced in our minds. To experience how this might feel, here's another exercise:

Think of a person or object.

Visualise this in your mind and focus for a few seconds on the image. – This image that you see might often be the way you are shown something by spirit – it will appear in your mind's eye.

Say a word to yourself in your head. Repeat the word. Can you 'hear' yourself in your mind saying this? – This is how it might feel when those in the spirit world give you a word, or how it might sound when spirit talks to you during a communication.

Think of something you like to cook. Can you smell it cooking? – This is what it might feel like when spirit gives you an odour.

Stroke your arm. Feel the sensation. – This can be what it feels like when spirit or your Spirit Guides want you to know they are near. This might also be how spirit want to draw attention to specific areas of the body. Spirit might do this to indicate which part of themselves was diseased and caused their death.

The only difference between your experiences above and your experience when you are communicating with spirit is that the word/image/thought will not have come from you but from outside yourself.

How does it feel to receive messages from spirit?

Have you ever noticed, when falling asleep that you see images in your mind's eye? Some people have described these to me as videos. I see them often as faces, one after another, each distinct but fleeting, as in the next second, another face appears.

Have you seen images, like post card scenes or photographs that just seem to jump into your mind from nowhere? This happens when you are in the hypnagogic state: that half-way state between wakefulness and sleep. This state has also been called a 'bridge to other realities'. It is while in this half-dreamlike state (when the mind drops censorship and is more open to suggestibility), that we are more likely to see visions.

Many mediums have described their experiences when connecting with spirit as being like these hypnagogic experiences. This exercise will help you feel what it is like to communicate with spirit.

Before going to bed, get out your Journal and write about something that is on your mind ... a problem or situation you are dealing with; a question or a dilemma.

Place a pad and paper by your bed and set the alarm for twenty minutes.

Try to clear your mind as you begin to fall asleep.

As you start to drift and feel yourself falling into the hypnagogic state, try to hold on to what comes to you.

If you fall asleep, your alarm will go off. When it does, keep whatever is in your mind and hold it there as you write it down immediately. Record all thoughts and images.

Later, you can consider what you have written, and decipher any symbols within.

You may not have been communicating with spirit during this exercise, but you will have been in touch with your Higher Self and this experience helps give you a feel of what it might be like for you to communicate with spirit.

Exercise with a Partner

Learning with a partner helps you to connect with your Spirit Guides while practising with someone you trust, in a relaxed frame of mind. When you are relaxed, this is different to meditating, as you are now 'working with' your guides.

Ground and shield.

Close your eyes and breathe in; breathe out. As you breathe out, visualise yourself breathing out a colour (your choice of colour) that fills your aura and surrounds you.

Now ask your Spirit Guide to come close to you and feel them come into your aura. Feel your guide enter your aura and recognise the change in energy. If you know your guide's calling card, wait until this is shown to you.

Try to feel your guide but if you can't, know that you have asked for them to come close and trust they are there.

Now ask your guide to give you a message, word or image that you can pass on to your partner. You might see something flash into your mind, get a feeling, hear words in your head or see a scene.

Next, ask your Spirit Guide how to interpret what you have been given in a way that will be helpful for your partner – be patient – your guide will communicate with you in their own way and this will be personal to you and your guide. They might show you a memory of yours, a person you know, an object that you can relate to or a song that has meaning to you and this may help you link the association of your first message so you can pass this on to your partner. Stay relaxed and visualise the colour that fills your aura slowly receding.

Thank your guide for working with you and pass on the message to your partner.

Student Response

Student 1: *My colour that I chose to fill my aura with was pink. I'm being drawn, when I think of this, to your heart chakra, to all the love you give out to others but feel I want to tell you that you are worthy of your love too and of some pampering. This also seems to relate to what I was given by my guides. I was given a Children's Nursery Rhyme book and when asked how to interpret this for you, was given that it is by Robert Louise Stevenson which takes me to memories of this book that I loved when I was a child. The poetry was so imaginative, the illustrations would transport my mind to wonderful places. I feel there is so much in this message for you. I'm feeling a love of books when you were a child: that wonderful excitement of opening a new book, not knowing where it was going to take you. The smell of new books even, would add to this sense of adventure and imagination. I feel that you are being reminded of how great it feels to lose yourself in imagination and creativity. I feel you are being prompted to try to re-connect with your inner child. I want to add to this because I was also given the poem "Faster than fairies, faster than witches, bridges, houses, hedges and ditches" ... it goes something like that and it is so fast paced and I found it quite magical as a child but for you, now, I feel it is a summary of your lifestyle: fast paced, constant, busy ... and although you're doing a lot, I feel, within your family, it is always in 'adult', 'mother', 'grandmother', 'housewife' mode. Even when reading to the children, it's like you don't have time to connect with your inner-child. I feel this message is reminding you to relax and remember that great sensation of awe and wonder, excitement and anticipation that children feel and often we grow out of. It's still there waiting for you to tap into it and I feel this might be really good for you. I hope this makes sense to you.*

Student 2 response: *I smiled when you gave me this message as I'm amazed by how similar it is to the one I have for you! Yes, I resonate very much to this and felt the message was meaningful for me ⋯ so amazing indeed! For you, the colour I chose to fill my aura was green and I saw woods, and when asked for interpretation I thought of Rumplestiltskin but then felt as though the woods and nature brings you to a state of relaxation and rest ... like walking on air; no worries or cares while strolling in nature .... You are most relaxed by it and as peaceful as Rumple is in his slumber. –*

Student 1 Reply: *Your words have sent shivers down my spine. I feel you have a really good connection. I love walking through woods, love trees and other than the sea, this is where I feel closest to nature and to the Universe. I loved fairy tales ... they too inspired me when I was young and I so believe in the magic of the fairy world. I know I loved that fairy tale when I was young and can hardly remember it now so I'm going to read it because all your words resonated with me, too ... thank you – it seems like we both need to reconnect with our inner child!*

Student 3: *My guides gave me an image of a group of people for my partner. I got the words "I like to be by myself," too. I feel you are a sociable lady who gets on with those you know very well. But I'm also getting that you like to be on your own at times too, so I feel some time alone is precious to you and also the times you are with other people? I hear laughter and happy talking going on. I feel you are a very caring lady.*

Student 4 response: *That sounds like me! I've been really enjoying my time alone, particularly these last few months and have also really enjoyed my time with family and friends too. I definitely care about people and the world in general so I feel this was a lovely message.*

Student 5: *The colour I chose for my aura was white. I feel my partner's angels are looking after her and she is well protected. I was given the names John, Joe and James relating to you and the number seven. I see a lot of grandchildren. I also feel you are a caring and loving mum and grandmother. Your children think the world of you and you of them. I am also hearing "take time out for yourself". You work hard too.*

Student 6 response: *This is lovely. The names are relevant and I do have four children and eight grandchildren who I dearly love. You are right, too, that I don't often take time for myself but I'm happiest cooking for my whole family with all the hustle and bustle around me. Thank you.*

Student 7: *The colour I chose is yellow. I was shown myself looking out over a field of yellow sunflowers and daffodils. This was shown to me in one of my meditations a while back and it has become my happy place. My guide wants me to share this with you and tell you to visualize miles of all these yellow flowers and just take in the beauty. Realize and feel just how much you have endured, how far you have come, and just how much there is to look forward to. I just heard "you are going places girl," and all you have to do is believe. That's it ... just believe. Imagine ... it's as simple as that. I feel so much peace now.*

Student 8 response to above: *That's so beautiful, thank you. I will hold this message close to my heart. I chose lilac as my aura, (my favourite peaceful colour). I got the smell of tobacco. I saw you as a young girl, smiling and running through a forest/wooded area, so happy. Is this a happy place for you or a memory you can connect to? I was also given a George Michael song "Amazing"; if you haven't heard it, can you listen to it as I think there's a message in there for you. – It's such a happy uplifting song with gorgeous words. It is being sent to you with love.*

Student 7 Response: *I just googled the words and I have to thank you because there are words in there that are resonating with some things going on. I have to listen to it later. One of his songs "Father Figure" I think is the name and every time I hear it, it just makes me feel a certain (good) way especially the pipe organ at the end! It really just takes me to another place and I have to stop and pause for a moment. It's funny because I was at an Estate sale over the weekend and I bought two things: a George (Washington) bottle and an old wooden picture of Arch Angel Michael and the singer's name you mention is George Michael! A coincidence...I think not! I actually felt like there was going to be some kind of connection with these two things as I was purchasing them. Love this!*

Student 8: *Thank you for your great and encouraging feedback.*

Student 7: *Feedback is so important when you are developing. It can be the very thing that gives you the nudge to keep moving and not give up. Not to say you will be 100% all the time, but you gotta cherish the times you are connecting to something higher than us and are being shown the proof. I am glad to be able to do that for you.*

Tutor: Signs come in many forms and always when they are needed. We just have to be open to notice them.

Working with Spirit 7 – Ethics and Responsibilities

When connecting and receiving messages from spirit, remember to ground, shield and cleanse with your own preferred methods for doing this. You can cleanse under your waterfall as many times a day as you wish. The more you do this, the easier you will find it to be under your waterfall in an instant. Protect yourself regularly.

Between each reading, ground, shield and protect.

Drink plenty of water when doing mediumship as it can dehydrate you. Remember to open and close before and after you start a mediumship session so you aren't open to spirit at all of the time and anywhere. Remember that you are the one in charge. When you are doing mediumship you have a responsibility to keep yourself safe and a responsibility towards your sitter.

Remember that words you pass on will remain with them and could have a big impact on their mind and emotions. For this reason, think about the words you use. It is not necessary to pass on everything you hear especially if you feel it might cause upset or harm to your sitter. Remember that those in the spirit world are just like us: ordinary people with personalities, who once had a life, family and friends they will still feel close to. Ordinary people can make mistakes and say the wrong thing at the wrong time. Not all spirits are so highly evolved that they are aware of the upset or hurt they might cause through saying the wrong thing. It is up to you to censor what you hear if you feel it will harm the person you are reading for, emotionally, or in any other way.

All mediums should have a set of ethics to operate under. These should include:

- Being honest and true to yourself, to spirit and to your sitter.
- To read without bias or prejudice.
- To respect all religions, beliefs and cultures and to read without being judgemental.
- Not to colour the reading with your own biases, views or theories and distort the link with spirit.
- When doing private readings to maintain total confidentiality.
- To pass on only information that has been given to you by spirit and to do this with decency, compassion and propriety. Never fabricate information.
- To be aware of the need to choose your words carefully when passing on information that might upset or hurt your sitter. I can't stress enough that diplomacy is vital when doing psychic and mediumship work.
- Psychics and mediums can offer healing but you should not try to diagnose health problems unless you are qualified to do so. It is illegal to treat anyone for an illness unless you are appropriately qualified. Health matters should not be discussed in depth. If you have concerns about someone's health, you might suggest (diplomatically) that they see their doctor.
- Never open yourself for mediumship under the influence of drugs or alcohol or while in an environment that makes you feel uneasy or that

might link you with anything that is negative, dark or harmful.

Working with Spirit 8 – Frequently Asked Questions and Group Discussions

Never be afraid to ask questions, for after all, this is how we learn. We have found, in our workshops that similar questions will be brought up regularly and I am including some of these in this Workbook for those of you who may have similar queries on your mind.

Frequently asked questions:

Student: We lost our dog six months ago and the other night I had a dream that he came to me. It felt so real. We walked together in the woods where I always walked him and he was so full of energy. I was so happy to see him again and felt both sad and happy when I woke up. Happy because the dream felt so real, sad because I miss him. Could my dog have visited me in this dream?

Tutor: Our pets and loved ones in spirit can and do visit us in our dreams. When we recall dreams of loved ones with such intensity and when they feel so real, trust that the visit was real and is such a blessing to hold on to. Your dog wants you to know he is okay and is with you.

Student: Who are my Spirit Guides?

Tutor: We all have a team of Spirit Guides who assist us on our spiritual journey and in the physical world. Some are with us all through our lives, others will come to us at certain times to help us through specific lessons. Each of our Spirit Guides will have lived many times before in the physical world and are now at a level to enable them to assist other souls on their spiritual journeys, here on earth. Just as we learn and grow, they will be very experienced and will have received a great deal of training to be able to assist us with the many challenges we face in our life.

Student: When I ask my Spirit Guides for answers and I receive more than one response, how do I know which one to listen to?

Tutor: It is likely that your first response is from your Higher Self or your Spirit Guide. Very quickly our minds can start questioning this or our 'thinking selves' will also answer. We all find this, so you aren't the only one. You might be doubting your intuitive skills, or feel fearful of trusting them and again, this happens to us all. Your ego might butt in and tell you to just believe and give what you get and your guides will be offering kind, helpful and non-judgemental advice.

So, for instance, if you asked, 'how can I trust my mediumship?', you might get answers like:

Your 'thinking mind': I am not a real medium, this is too hard

Your Ego: Give what you get and get on with it

Your Guides: Be kind to yourself and give yourself time. We are always here for you and will help you build your confidence and your mediumship skills.

It takes time to learn which one to listen to ⋯ time and practice ⋯ and the more you practice and pay attention to your guides' kind and loving guidance, the less you will notice negative thoughts and doubts.

Student: Is my Guardian Angel my Spirit Guide?

Tutor: Some people think our Guides and Guardian Angels are the same, others will differ in their views. Our Guides are spirits just like us who have lived many times before, completed their 'earthly' lessons and have had a lot of training in spirit to enable them to guide us on our journey through life. There are angels, too, who have lived before. I believe we have Angels that guard and protect us just like our Spirit Guides and although some people say our Angels are watching over many people while our Spirit Guides are personal to us and are with us every moment, I believe we have a Guardian Angel who is always with us, too, and often see my Guardian Angel also as my Protector Guide. I also feel our Spirit Guides can be shared and may be guiding others too. ⋯ Trust your own feelings on this.

GROUP DISCUSSION 1

Student 1: Hi everyone, with the permission of my tutor, I would like to put one of my readings forward for analysis. I will also give the feedback I received. My questions are: Do you feel this was a mediumship reading or an intuitive one? Could I have improved this reading? Please be truthful as I'd like to learn from this and hope others too will learn from this little exercise.

My reading: Angie, the moment you said "I could really be doing with my mum right now", my heart went out to you and I would like to try to read for you. I feel your mum just wants you to know that she hears you and is there for you. I feel your mum was a quiet child. She may have told you that she was quite shy when she was younger but her confidence grew and she was actually quite a sociable person. She had the type of personality that made people feel at ease in her company. I feel you may have felt, when you were younger, that you had to share her with so many others who always knew she'd be there for them but there was no competition really because her family would always come first. I feel she did quite well at school but she didn't like exams. She's talking about a test and I don't know if it was a driving test ... did someone struggle to pass their test and it became a bit of a joke in the family? She's talking about a blue car and trips to the seaside or to a special place you all enjoyed and now every time you go there or think about it, it can seem as if those memories were only moments ago. She's mentioning angels ... I feel you were her angel, her sweet little angel and you still are. This will never change. Does the year 1978 mean anything? Also the months February and October? I also feel she wants me to mention the twins or two people in the family who were born around the same time. Remember your mum is with you whenever you call on her to be with you. Love is eternal and never dies. Can you understand this?

FEEDBACK FOR THIS READING: I don't really know much about my mum as a child. I'm not sure about a test or the blue car but we did go to the seaside a lot with my aunt uncle and cousins. We were a close family. My mum was my best friend. I can't think of anything for 1978 or February but my dad's birthday was October and I have twins. (She did not thank me for the reading).

Tutor 1: How do you feel about this yourself? You had two specific pieces of evidence accepted: the twins and the month of October. Some of the personal feelings about Angie's mum could well be true but they can't be confirmed. Did you notice a difference in how you felt when you were given 'twins' for instance to when you felt her mum did quite well at school?

Student 1: As I start my readings, I always try to get a feel for the character of spirit who come through, I sense their nature and it feels tentative at first. Could this be a link or is it just me intuitively feeling this? I did feel a stronger energy as I continued and the twins: I heard twice 'twins' but again I wondered if this was intuitive. As I look back now I think maybe that's when the link was growing stronger but that's when I ended the reading. Maybe I should try to keep the connection open a bit longer and try to get more.

Student 2: You got so much information on the reading and mentioned dates and places. You also picked up on the twins which she confirmed that she had twins. I think it's a good reading.

Student 1. Thank you. There was also the test and blue car but maybe they are memories that couldn't be confirmed by the sitter.

Tutor 1: I did think that this reading is okay if she knows about her mum's childhood which seemingly from the feedback she didn't. The validation of twins is great and the beach days too. I feel starting off a reading on a negative is setting yourself up for a fall. Before you start doubting yourself, which in turn, may not give her much confidence in you i.e. 'I would like to try', say 'I would like to read for you'. I also feel any softer things are best left until further into the reading as when you gave the words 'My heart went out to you', I feel this could indicate you are feeling sorry for Angie, as opposed to really making a connection, although you clearly did and having said this, the reading flows when you go with the flow. No two readings are the same. She was very blunt but we, none of us, are the same.

Tutor 2: I agree with Tutor 1 that the feedback was blunt and maybe she was looking for something specific that meant she immediately dismissed anything she couldn't instantly verify. It's often the case that some things need to be validated by another family member.

Student 1: Great advice. I went straight in with a negative didn't I! And with feeing so nervous, I approached the reading warily as if dipping my toe in with a clear lack of confidence. It makes me feel good that you thought it was mediumship though as maybe I am linking in which means working on it should help improve it. Possibly too, the twins could have been my link to building the energy, had she been more cooperative.

Tutor 1: Sometimes you can ease your sitter into a softer frame of mind if they feel, from you, the same.

Tutor 2: I feel some of this is more intuitive than mediumship. I am led to believe that everyone we meet is said to leave an energy imprint of some sort on our aura. The more of an impact they have in our lives, the greater the influence on our aura. Therefore, as a psychic as well as a medium, we can tune into the auric field and work on a psychic link. This would mean no contact with a spirit person, the information coming from the recipient and their aura only. So, although memories of her mother's childhood may have been via mediumship, it doesn't necessarily mean it should be taken as such. For instance, the childhood memories are too generalised and could be accepted by most people as being from their mother. I agree that the delivering of information that cannot be accepted at the time of a reading and then later validated is great mediumship as this proves the medium could not have picked it up from the aura of the sitter but from a spirit communicator.

Student 3: A lovely reading but because you started with 'I feel your mum wants you to know,' rather than 'I feel I have your mum here. She is showing me blah blah features, blah blah height etc, or she is telling me blah blah, it sounds like intuitive but it could just be your empathy coming out and the strong emotional link. Then you are definitely linked in as she is showing you memories either clairvoyantly or making you feel clairsentient, then you mention dates, etc. Very abrupt feedback that makes me feel she wants something specific.

Student 1: Thank you all, for your advice and thoughts. This kind of confirms my own feelings on this. I shall keep on trying and will maybe, in a few months' time, give another reading to compare with this one, to see if we can notice any progress.

Student 2: I loved this discussion as it has helped me a lot.

Tutor 2: I feel the following applies to Student 1 as much as it does to us all when doing readings. I feel we are all learning in mediumship. We are not here to rest on our laurels as this isn't helpful nor is it progress so my words aren't to hinder, judge or offend here. Please feel free to dismiss them all. Regarding your reading, Student 1, this information you receive will come through whatever clair happens to be strongest within you and this will change the more you go forward in your mediumship. There are some things you could have done to improve your delivery – believe me, we all say this after readings. The message you gave Angie was in all fairness, fine, although it might have been preferable to have asked Spirit for more personal evidence. This would allow for a degree of scepticism to be minimised from your sitter. It would also raise your confidence in knowing you have a Spirit link and it is not your own mind interfering. Remember, we are in control of our mediumship at all times and we will get out of it what we put into it. You told Angie that her mum had the type of personality that people felt at ease with..... These are very nice words to hear but they do not describe her personality. Would you agree if I said they are general and could apply to anyone? Your aim as a medium is to describe to the sitter her mother's personality and character to help prove you are communicating to her loved one. This is achieved only by asking questions of the Spirit. What were her likes and dislikes, her hobbies and could she have a Jekyll and Hyde personality? Could she be trusted? Was she honest in her dealing or a scoundrel in disguise?

You gave "She's talking about a blue car and trips to the seaside or to a special place...." expand on this, again. Ask questions to help validation come forward. The blue of the car could be your symbol for healing taking place at a beach outing or special trip. Ask for specific memories that they have shared together.

The twins were known to Angie as being her own children so you could have picked this up from her or you could have received it from her mum. It's been my experience that Spirit don't give us information without a reason, so, ask her mum why she has mentioned them. If you get no answer it could be your own mind putting it there but why? Listen to your intuition and let it guide you to the answer. It may be Angie is worried or concerned about one of them for a good reason, if so which one? What gender are the twins? – you don't know so ask. The answers will come in time and through practice.

GROUP DISCUSSION 2

Tutor 1: Mediumship Scenario – okay, how would you give a reading if you were faced with a sitter who is listening to your every word and you are picking up that they are in a violent relationship. How would you word it? Would you say anything?

Student 1: This is a good question to think about and difficult too. The way I would respond to this would depend on who the sitter is, their personality and the nature of the relationship they are in. I would respond to this with my instinct and my heart. I might say "I feel you are in a situation at the moment that is extremely difficult and upsetting but due to your circumstances it's not easy to escape or resolve the issue. In this situation, most people would tell you to do one thing but it's not always easy for it is taking a lot of strength to go through this. It also makes you feel trapped, scared and frustrated about the issue. I feel you are less inclined to talk about the issue to close friends and family." ··· I wasn't direct here. I could have just said it like "I feel you are in a violent relationship" but I don't' think that's the way. That is my answer but an average answer as it would depend on the sitter and their response. The sitter may have told me by now this was the case and want to open up about it. Sometimes people go to mediums and psychics because they can't talk to people around them in difficult situations and they have no one to talk to. They might be relieved you pick up on these things and more importantly, they might need an answer or some guidance.

Tutor 1: As mediums we are not tuning into the sitter but to spirit, although they may show us that the person in front of us is in a violent relationship. I once saw the father of my sitter standing between her and another person as if protecting her and in saying this, she was the one who brought up the hostility in her relationship.

Student 2: If I were picking up a feeling they are in an abusive relationship, I would feel morally obligated to open the gate if they needed someone to come to for 'help'. I'd probably say I'm getting a strong feeling they may be experiencing a difficult relationship and ask if this made sense to them. I might say that sometimes they may question whether to remain in the relationship or to let go. Depending on their reply, would steer me where to go with the reading. If they seem ready to talk about it, I might suggest a professional they could turn to. If I felt they didn't want to talk, I would move on to another subject.

Student 3: Depending on how the sitter is during the reading, or if they ask anything, I would mention something like 'I feel the relationship is changing and it isn't as good as it once was. Your loved ones' in spirit are letting you know they are around you, protecting you as they are able and sending you some healing to give you the strength at this time, to talk to someone if needed at any time in the future and then say things more positive too.'

Tutor 2: This is a situation where a medium has to use tact and diplomacy to discreetly pass information to a sitter. If spirit are communicating, they usually express their thoughts in a way that will not cause further hurt or pain. They will let the sitter know they are around them and being supportive as much as they can be. In the above scenario, it's likely to be our psychic faculty that is giving us the impression of on-going events in their life and not spirit relaying it. I would want to come across as being compassionate towards their issues rather than appearing abrupt. No medium or psychic can solve people's issues but we can suggest to them to contact those who are qualified in whichever area, to find the right help and support. I imagine most people in this type of situation will carry feelings of shame and failure so it's important to aim to be positive in our wordings and not judge any one person or the situation.

Working with Spirit 9 – Delivering the Message

All mediums have their own way to connect with spirit and with experience you will find you develop your own. Putting what you have learned so far into practise, will help cleanse, ground and protect you while working with spirit and you will have control over your mediumship so you aren't left feeling drained. We offer advice and guidance and you can choose which of our teachings apply in your own work and which to discard.

You have come so far already and this is just the start of a beautiful journey into mediumship. There is still much to learn and experience and indeed for myself as well and I look forward to this as I hope you do, too. For this Workbook, all that is left is for me to remind you of the responsibility you have as a medium.

Mediumship and working with the public is a big responsibility. As a medium you are a conduit between our world and the afterlife, bringing messages of hope and comfort to those who need it. You may be helping people who are grieving to heal. As has already been discussed, your words can have a big impact on your sitter and for this reason, you need to be very aware of the need to word your message in a way that does bring comfort.

As already discussed, some mediums will insist that they will 'give what they get' as if there is something 'important' in having to deliver messages in this way. Is it ego, a lack of compassion or a lack of consideration for the feelings of their sitter that prompts them to read in this way? Whatever the reason, there are some vital points to consider when you are, as a medium, providing a service for the public. You have responsibilities and there are laws to protect clients who receive a service from others.

You should never pass on messages or information that might harm someone you are reading for. People who seek mediumship services are grieving and are likely to be emotionally vulnerable. You aren't being untrue to spirit if you have to deliver messages in a more comforting, uplifting way than how they are received. You are being considerate of your sitter. You might work with your Spirit Guides from the start so they can help filter information you would prefer not to know in order to help you pass on comforting words and meaningful evidence to your sitters.

In our work, we have seen mediums upset families by suggesting 'suicide' when this was not at all the case, mediums who passed on gory details which left lasting, upsetting impressions on the sitter and one medium who told a woman (after a lot of leading questions) that her step-daughter was thieving from her. This made the woman quite angry toward the younger girl who turned out to be quite innocent ⋯ the medium had pieced information together through a series of questions, came up with the wrong conclusion and wasn't passing on messages from spirit but from his own egotistical need to feel important.

As a medium, be true to your clients, to yourself and to spirit by learning to know your own mind and know the difference between information coming from spirit and from your own mind and imagination.

I hope you have enjoyed your journey so far and wish you many magical experiences as you find your own unique approach to receiving and giving messages from the spirit world.

Carole Anne

Made in the USA
Coppell, TX
13 January 2021